"*Authentic Excellence* has been transf[...] assuredly for individual students who learn [...] lence through the lens of personal values, bu[...] [...]greater university community where we are talking now more than ever about resilience, integrative wellness, and human flourishing."

Virginia M. Ambler, Ph.D., Vice President for
Student Affairs, William & Mary

"*Authentic Excellence* is a must read not only for young adults who want to flourish and thrive in life but also for the educators, friends and families who want to support them on their journey. Focusing on a values-based approach, this book is an excellent resource for all of us who are trying to lead fulfilling and purposeful lives."

Sue Wasiolek, J.D., Associate Vice President for
Student Affairs and Dean of Students, Duke University

"Fear of failure so often paralyzes our growth, personally and professionally. *Authentic Excellence* offers the rare combination of wisdom and practical strategies for becoming our best selves, guided by values. It is essential reading for young adults who want to reach their potential in a rapidly changing world."

Christopher Adkins, Ph.D., Professor and Director of the
Deloitte Center for Ethical Leadership, University of Notre Dame

"Simply put, this book will help you lead a high quality, meaningful life. It's tough out there, but *Authentic Excellence* shows you how to manage fear, adopt a resilient mindset and how to flourish. It is one of those rare books that will have a positive, long-lasting influence on your life."

Ken White, Ph.D., Associate Dean, MBA & Executive Programs,
Raymond A. Mason School of Business, William & Mary

"There is no greater gift you can give yourself than to view life's choices through the lens of values. Early adulthood comes with many stressful decisions. *Authentic Excellence* shares a proven values-centered approach that empowers you to thrive vs. languish through your journey of gaining independence and leading your life where you want it to go."

Joni Fedders, President, Aileron Institute

Authentic Excellence

Never before have the pressures of a comparative and competitive world impacted more on our sense of wellbeing, particularly among young adults. Building on the principles of Giving Voice to Values, which honors the complexity and difficulty of leading with our values, this book addresses the unique challenges faced by young adults. It provides a clear process that details how to harness natural wisdom to flourish through the relentless pace and pressure of today's world. Moving beyond mere values clarification, *Authentic Excellence* helps the reader to develop a deeper relationship with their values and confidently express them, and builds effective coping skills to manage the relentless noise of our comparative and competitive world.

Authentic Excellence answers five primary questions:

- How are young adults affected by this world of relentless change and pressure?
- Why are young adults vulnerable to a plateau that can negatively affect their resilience?
- What is the difference between fear-based excellence and authentic excellence and what role do values play in this distinction?
- What is necessary to move beyond fear-based excellence and why is it so hard?
- How do you train a deeper level of effectiveness that includes more consistent productivity, fulfillment and resilience?

R. Kelly Crace is Associate Vice President for Health & Wellness at William & Mary, Williamsburg, VA, and Director of the Center for Mindfulness and Authentic Excellence (CMAX). He has served as director of two college mental health centers at Duke University and William & Mary. He is a licensed psychologist and co-author of the *Life Values Inventory*.

Robert Louis Crace is Executive Director of the non-profit Life Values Inventory Online, Inc. He consults with creatives and young adults on concepts of values, flourishing, and resilience.

Giving Voice to Values
Series Editor: Mary C. Gentile

The *Giving Voice to Values* series is a collection of books on Business Ethics and Corporate Social Responsibility that brings a practical, solutions-oriented, skill-building approach to the salient questions of values-driven leadership.

Giving Voice to Values (GVV; www.GivingVoiceToValues.org) – the curriculum, the pedagogy and the research upon which it is based – was designed to transform the foundational assumptions upon which the teaching of business ethics is based, and importantly, to equip future business leaders to know not only what is right – but how to make it happen.

Giving Voice to Values in the Legal Profession
Carolyn Plump

Giving Voice to Values in Accounting
Tara J. Shawver and William F. Miller

Giving Voice to Values as a Professional Physician
Ira Bedzow

Authentic Excellence
R. Kelly Crace and Robert Louis Crace

Authentic Excellence

Flourishing and Resilience in a Relentless World

R. Kelly Crace and Robert Louis Crace

LONDON AND NEW YORK

First published 2020
by Routledge
2 Park Square, Milton Park, Abingdon, Oxon OX14 4RN

and by Routledge
52 Vanderbilt Avenue, New York, NY 10017

Routledge is an imprint of the Taylor & Francis Group, an informa business

British Library Cataloguing-in-Publication Data
A catalogue record for this book is available from the British Library

Library of Congress Cataloging-in-Publication Data
Names: Crace, R. Kelly, author. | Crace, Robert Louis, author.
Title: Authentic excellence / R. Kelly Crace and Robert Louis Crace.
Description: Abingdon, Oxon ; New York, NY : Routledge, 2019. |
Includes bibliographical references and index.
Identifiers: LCCN 2019007719 | ISBN 9780367151355 (hardback) |
ISBN 9780367151379 (pbk.) | ISBN 9780429055270 (ebook)
Subjects: LCSH: Youth–Conduct of life. | Values. | Self-realization.
Classification: LCC BJ1661 .C678 2019 | DDC 170/.44–dc23
LC record available at https://lccn.loc.gov/2019007719

ISBN: 978-0-367-15135-5 (hbk)
ISBN: 978-0-367-15137-9 (pbk)
ISBN: 978-0-429-05527-0 (ebk)

Typeset in Times New Roman
by Newgen Publishing UK

Graphic illustrations and cover design by Keith Johnson and Kevin Crace

Contents

Foreword

Mary C. Gentile
University of Virginia Darden School of Business; author of Giving Voice to Values: How to Speak Your Mind When You Know What's Right

In *Authentic Excellence*, R. Kelly Crace and Robert Louis Crace have provided a compelling and impactful roadmap to self-insight, empowerment and values-driven satisfaction for young adults. This map will be a powerful tool for those who work with this population—teachers, counselors, parents, mentors—and for young adults themselves.

I am delighted and honored to include this offering in the *Giving Voice to Values* (GVV) book series. GVV is an innovative approach and methodology for values-driven leadership development that was originally developed for business students and practitioners. However, its practical and empowering approach to ethical action has led to its adoption across professions and around the world over the past decade.

GVV is not about persuading people to be more ethical. Rather, GVV starts from the premise that most of us already want to act on our values, but that we also want to feel that we have a reasonable chance of doing so effectively and successfully. This pedagogy and curriculum are about raising those odds.

Rather than a focus on ethical analysis, the GVV curriculum focuses on ethical implementation and asks the questions "What if I were going to act on my values? What would I say and do? How could I be most effective?"

As I share GVV around the world and across contexts both educational and professional, I find that almost every time I speak about this empowering approach to enacting our values, someone will ask: Can we use this approach with our children? And with young adults? I have always answered in the affirmative, sharing anecdotes from educators and managers who have shared personal stories about how they have utilized this methodology with their own families. And then I follow with an invitation—strongly felt—for interested individuals to help develop an application of GVV for the youth audience— an application that precedes our professional roles and focuses on the actual formation of effective, confident, competent values-driven individuals.

Now with *Authentic Excellence*, Kelly and Bobby Crace have created a wonderful handbook for those who want to help guide and empower youth to their empowered and confident values-driven futures. Based on their own data and extensive experience with college youth, they have identified the ways in which our own values, goals, and talents—our very best characteristics—can sometimes get in our own way and set up obstacles to growth and happiness. They outline the common pitfalls that young adults can encounter, ironically often as a result of their own early achievements. They become afraid of falling behind, of not being able to match their own (and others') expectations, of failing. Or they become so focused on external metrics of success that they lose the joy and delight in their own abilities.

Crace and Crace offer a set of self-assessment questions as well as practical and manageable steps for moving forward at each stage of development, helping young adults to find the pleasure and satisfaction in learning again, in growing again, in accepting setbacks as signs of progress and guideposts toward development rather than as devastating failures. Their book is replete with recognizable stories of young adults at various stages of development and life challenges, with strategies for working through them.

The authors' wise guidance reflects many of the pillars and lessons of GVV: the "normalization" of challenge, of fear and of difficult emotions; the power in self-knowledge and playing to one's own strengths; the acceptance and the valuing of a growth mindset—the journey toward ever-increasing effectiveness in expressing our values—as opposed to a success or failure, win or lose approach to life's challenges.

Perhaps most importantly, *Authentic Excellence* affirms that we all—especially young adults—have more choices when it comes to living out our highest values than our fears and insecurities sometimes lead us to think. This insight is key to not only individual satisfaction and happiness but to a better world for all of us.

Acknowledgments

We'd like to thank Mary Gentile for providing the opportunity to express our values work in book form. Dr. Gentile's seminal work in empowering people to lead with their values has given voice to our work by including *Authentic Excellence* in her *Giving Voice to Values* book series. We'd also like to thank her for her direction in editing and developing this book.

Thank you to Rebecca Marsh at Routledge for her guidance throughout the publishing process. To Keith Johnson and Kevin Crace whose cover design and graphic work has helped bring the important concepts of this book to life, thank you. We'd also like to thank Andrew Rosen for his tireless work in designing LVIO.org and the Life Values Inventory hard copy assessment in Appendix A.

The thirty plus years of work and research in developing the Life Values Inventory (LVI) and Authentic Excellence Initiative would not be possible without several facets of support and contribution. Thank you to Duane Brown, Charles Hardy, and Phil Meilman for their research partnership and professional mentoring, and to William & Mary, Duke University, and the University of North Carolina at Chapel Hill for the institutional platform our research and clinical work relied upon. We are also grateful to Sue Wasiolek & Sam Sadler for their administrative support of the LVI, and to Ginger Ambler for her mentoring in organizational flourishing and advocacy in building the Center for Mindfulness & Authentic Excellence at William & Mary. We also thank Marathon Consulting for their work in developing LVIO.org and creating one of the most sophisticated databases for values research available.

Special thanks to the Mathile family whose support in making the LVI an open educational resource to the general public has helped grow values research, promote values-based flourishing, and provided a platform of values work that is more inclusive.

We are thankful for our partners, Cindy and Maya, who have been vital sources of encouragement, wisdom, and resilience throughout this work.

This work is dedicated to R. Joseph Crace, the patriarch of flourishing and resilience in our family; the support of Teddie and Jerry Gause; and the loving memory of Bobby Dell'Orso, Rita Crace, Joe B. Crace, and Margaret Amodio, whose lives and stories were inspirational influences in the creation of this work.

Part I

Understanding the plateau effect

1 Introduction

Flourishing and resilience
in a relentless world

Anna is a sophomore in college. By all accounts, she is the model of success. She was popular in high school, valedictorian, an All-State Basketball player, actively involved in community service, and devoted to her family's faith community. Anna was seen as the rising star in her small town, and despite her family's financial struggles, her academic and athletic success led to many college opportunities. When she was accepted into a prominent university on a full scholarship, her small hometown celebrated as if her success was their success. She could rarely go anywhere without a community member sharing what her success meant to them. "Make us proud" became the normal "goodbye". While embarrassed to receive such attention, Anna accepted the pressure with a sense of honor and duty.

Despite being a first-generation college student, the transition to college went surprisingly smooth. The support and resources provided by the school and athletics team set her up to succeed. She respected her coach and felt fairly treated. She had good teammates who became her new group of friends. Her classes were tough but not beyond her capabilities. By the end of her freshman year, she had experienced the same level of success as in previous years.

Now, in the middle of the fall semester of her sophomore year, things had shifted dramatically. She was struggling to find motivation. She had never worried about initiative before and now was questioning everything. Her thoughts and actions were preoccupied with the question "why?". She started reexamining her family's faith, which had previously been a resource of strength. Her friends and teammates began to notice a change in her mood. She was not performing as well as she normally had on the court and in class. She regularly felt hurried but found little meaning in her busyness. Anna wished she could return to the "cruise control" she had felt in previous years, but doing things out of honor and duty was no longer enough. Her lack of motivation and constant questioning sparked feelings of selfishness and shame. She ended every day with negative self-judgment followed by proclamations like, "Tomorrow I will make up for today," only to wake up feeling overwhelmed and anxious.

This book is devoted to young adults like Anna who are in their late teens or twenties (aged 17–29). Today's emerging and young adults possess an incredible amount of talent and wisdom, but they are also vulnerable because of how something wonderful about them correlates to the current world in which they live. Essentially, emerging adults today want more than success; they want to be successful in something meaningful to them. However, the competition for those meaningful opportunities has never been more fierce. While young adults have been taught to strive for what is meaningful, managing the uncertainty that surrounds meaning and what is important to them is underemphasized.

Many young adults of previous generations carried the belief that if they were responsible and worked hard, opportunities would be available. Many felt that there was enough time to adjust, adapt, and even enjoy the efforts associated with transitioning to adulthood. **Trust exceeded fear.**

Not in today's world.

The relentless pace and uncertainty of our current world creates a life of ongoing and often overlapping change. Growing up, many young adults experienced the structuring of play and over-involvement in activities because of increased competition for academic and career opportunities. The "portfolio-building" culture of young people was intended to provide choices that led to success and happiness. But the consequence of a portfolio culture is that each transitional step has incredible implications for future opportunities. This pressure paired with a relentless pace of constant change creates a serious dilemma as it pertains to resilience.

All change, even positive change, has some level of loss and uncertainty. During transitions we're always leaving something, and what's ahead has some uncertainty attached to it. Our brain doesn't neutrally respond to this loss and uncertainty. We tend to have some form of reaction to what we're leaving and some form of worry or fear over the uncertainty of what's ahead. Depending on how confident you are with these emotions, change can be experienced as a time of stress and excitement, or a time of disruptive sadness and anxiety.

Fortunately, our nervous system is made to adapt to change. We are wired for crisis and regulation. Change is interpreted as a mini-crisis that we gear up for, and once through the transition we immediately seek a state of regulation and comfort. But today, it can feel like we get through one important change and barely have time to brace ourselves for the next wave of loss and uncertainty. Because we are experiencing more change before we gain a sense of confidence and rhythm, **fear is now exceeding trust.**

The result of this shift to relentless pace and pressure is that we tend to "live at our neurology". "Living at your neurology" means we are essentially using our sympathetic (crisis) and parasympathetic (regulation) nervous system as a motivational strategy. We focus on all of our critical "have to"s of the day and then seek comfort by whatever soothing habits we've developed. While this approach is natural and can be effective, it is a coping mechanism that starts to gradually erode our resilience, performance, and health.

It is important to understand what a relentless world has done to the dynamic relationship between trust and fear, how it has impacted resilience, and how it has created a plateau effect where young adults are vulnerable to staying "stuck at good". Eventually, certain patterns of managing pressure and fear can level off in terms of effectiveness. We can periodically achieve positive or "good" outcomes while living at our neurology, but eventually side effects such as burnout, overwhelming stress, chronic worry, apathy, and performance slumps begin to work against us. This book will explore factors that lead to the plateau effect and how to overcome those factors.

Authentic Excellence: What's in a name?

What is the message of the Authentic Excellence Initiative? Because young adults are inclined to strive for something meaningful but are not taught how to manage the uncertainties associated with doing so, they are vulnerable to a plateau effect. The very same reasons that lead emerging adults to excel through adolescence will start to work against them and carry increasing costs. The transition to adulthood can be a wonderful opportunity to break the natural pattern of thinking and behavior that fosters this plateau effect, rather than allowing this natural pattern to become more deeply entrenched.

The term "Authentic Excellence" reflects a redefinition of excellence based on one's sense of purpose derived from one's values rather than from outcomes experienced. By defining success as the courage to act on your values, you shift your basis of motivation and decision-making from being fear-centered to values-centered. This results in a deeper level of productivity, fulfillment, and resilience.

The name Authentic Excellence also highlights an important paradox of success. People often remark that while authenticity and values are great concepts, they don't change the fact that in this world, success is measured by outcomes. They're right. We can't ignore the reality of outcomes and the importance that they play in our world. Outcomes aren't bad; they actually carry several positive benefits. Outcomes can be used for motivation; they can give us feedback about our performance and they can serve as a reward for our hard work. But when we look at the factors that increase the probability of attaining outcomes, we see that our mindset about outcomes is critical. There is a difference between being outcome-driven and outcome-desperate. Essentially, when an outcome is a "want to" it tends to work positively for us; but when an outcome is a "need to" where it is attached to our self-worth, it tends to interfere with our performance. The name Authentic Excellence is intended to remind us that our performance is enhanced and optimized when we are engaged in authentic expression of our values.

How do we define flourishing in the context of Authentic Excellence? It is a consistent level of productivity, fulfillment, and resilience that stems from values-centered motivation, action, and management. This then begs the question, "What are values?" Our empirically based values assessment, the Life Values Inventory (Crace & Brown, 2012), defines values as basic set of beliefs that guide our motivation, decision-making, and behavior. They also serve as the lens for how we evaluate ourselves and others.

The Authentic Excellence Initiative focuses on five primary questions:

- How are young adults affected by this world of relentless change and pressure?
- Why are young adults vulnerable to a plateau that can negatively affect their resilience?
- What role do values play in distinguishing between fear-based excellence and authentic excellence?
- What is necessary to move beyond fear-based excellence and why is it so hard?
- How do you train toward a deeper level of effectiveness that includes more consistent productivity, fulfillment, and resilience?

There are many who view resilience as a quality one either possesses or does not. Most young adults have had to manage some hardship and have progressed successfully to their next life transition. Overall, humans are a resilient species and the more you study hardship, loss, and trauma, the more appreciative you become of how resilient we are. Even the most ineffective forms of coping require some measure of resilience. Our focus is to establish an awareness of one's current level of resilience and then advance the quality of that resilience.

We have also found that less resilience is not due to a lack of knowledge. In our assessment of healthy practices, we find that young adults are generally aware of what they need to do to live healthy, effective lives. They know about time and energy management, stress management, healthy choices about sleep, exercise, goal setting, etc. But knowledge is not enough. Something is getting in the way of acting on those behaviors.

This book is divided into three parts. Part I, "Understanding the plateau effect", explores why we have a natural tendency to plateau or stay "stuck at good". Part II, "Understanding and training for Authentic Excellence", guides you through the Five Paradigm Shifts that are essential for flourishing, and how to implement those strategies in your life. Part III, "Special considerations for flourishing and resilience", explores specific issues that can significantly impact flourishing, expression, and resilience. The subjects in Part III are specialized applications of the Authentic Excellence training that include sensitivity, creativity, transition, decision-making, leadership, and team development. Moving beyond mere values clarification, the Authentic Excellence Initiative helps you develop a deeper relationship with your values, teaches you how to confidently express and manage your values, and builds effective coping skills to manage the noise of your comparative and competitive world.

The concepts

The Authentic Excellence Initiative stems from an empirically derived values assessment process that focuses on principles of values-centered leadership and wellness. It is based on three decades of empirical and qualitative research, clinical practice, and consulting work concerning the relationship between values and effectiveness. It has included the study of clients from diverse socio-economic backgrounds and identities, ranging from high school to retirement age, from organizations within sport, business, academic, and government settings. Our research involved three different phases: (1) empirically derived values assessment, (2) understanding the relationship between values and flourishing, and (3) the assessment of a values-centered training model. This section briefly summarizes these phases.

Our earliest work explored how values could impact the navigation of important life transitions. During this time, we identified several methodological concerns involving how values were being assessed (Crace, 1992; Brown & Crace, 1996a). Concerns included a restrictive scope of assessment to either the rating or ranking of values; cultural and gender sensitivity; unclear distinction between aspirational values, operational values, and virtues; the use of open-ended projective questions that were often affected by mood to infer values; bias toward values infusion instead of values clarification; lack of attention to life roles and their relationship to values; and poor psychometric properties. We began a ten-year empirical exploration of values to address these methodological concerns. Our research included a diverse sample of students from high schools, community colleges, and universities, as well as adult workers. We used a sequential systems analysis approach, applying a stringent series of exploratory and confirmatory factor analyses; reliability analyses using test-retest and internal consistency coefficients; validity tests using convergent, divergent, and predictive validity analyses; and two rounds of cultural and gender sensitivity reviews. The result was the Life Values Inventory (LVI), which accounted for over 75% of the total variance and demonstrated incremental validity over extant values assessments (Brown & Crace, 1996a, 2002; Crace, 1992; Crace & Brown, 1996, 1997, 2002a, 2006, 2012). Other previously identified assessment concerns were addressed by including both crystallization and prioritization of values and the interaction of values with behavior, and assessing how values are expressed through life roles. We continue to refine the psychometric properties of this assessment through ongoing analyses of a growing database of over 160,000 subjects (www.lifevaluesinventory.org).

Starting from a list of almost 200 values from previous values research, the following 14 values emerged as the most stable empirically.

It is important for me to…

- challenge myself and work hard to improve (**Achievement**);
- be accepted by others and feel included (**Belonging**);
- protect and preserve the environment (**Concern for the Environment**);
- help and attend to the wellbeing of others (**Concern for Others**);
- have new ideas, create new works, or be creatively expressive (**Creativity**);
- be financially successful (**Financial Prosperity**);

- be healthy and physically active (**Health and Activity**);
- be humble and modest about my accomplishments (**Humility**);
- have a sense of autonomy with my decisions and actions (**Independence**);
- honor the expectations of my family, social group, team, or organization (**Interdependence**);
- use logical principles to understand and solve problems (**Objective Analysis**);
- have time alone (**Privacy**);
- be dependable and trustworthy (**Responsibility**);
- have spiritual beliefs that reflect being a part of something greater than myself (**Spirituality**).

Concurrent with this assessment research, there were two additional phases of inquiry: (1) exploring the role that values play in managing life transitions, life role development, team development, resilience, and performance effectiveness (Brown & Crace, 1996b, 1997a, 1997b, 2002, 2008; Brown, Crace, & Almeida, 2006; Crace, 2005, 2007, 2008, 2010a, 2010b, 2011a, 2011b, 2012a, 2012b, 2013a, 2013b, 2013c; Crace & Brown, 1997, 2002a, 2002b; Crace & Hardy, 1996, 1997; Crace & Ivy, 2011; Crace & Lickerman, 2014; Hardy, Burke, & Crace, 2005; Hardy & Crace, 1991, 1993, 1997; Hardy, Crace, & Burke, 1999; Meilman, Crace, Presley, & Lyerla, 1995; Silva & Crace, 1987; Silva, Hardy, & Crace, 1988); and (2) developing and evaluating the effectiveness of a mental training program that sought to improve individual and organizational flourishing (Crace, 2017; Crace & Lickerman, 2014).

We adopted a qualitative research paradigm to utilize the rich data obtained from in-depth interviews in clinical, academic, and consulting settings. The individuals interviewed were clients who spanned the full range of functioning from languishing to flourishing. At first, our efforts were focused on individuals who were going through important life transitions, including planned transitions (e.g., the transition to college or graduate school, starting a first job, mid-career change, or retirement) and unplanned transitions (e.g., injury, illness, or loss). Two particularly fascinating groups included elite athletes and performing artists who had experienced career-threatening or career-ending injuries, and women who were transitioning to or from high-level STEM field professions. In our counseling sessions with these individuals we began to see the impact that values could have on their resilience. We developed an interview that assessed client perceptions of flourishing as it pertained to productivity, fulfillment, and resilience in each of their life roles. The aim of the interviews was to understand the factors that contributed to periods when they were flourishing, as well as those that interfered with flourishing. Understanding these factors within life roles was critical in that individuals were often flourishing in one role but not in other life roles. To the degree that the relationship with clients spanned over a period of time, longitudinal interviews were conducted over time. As the psychometric properties of the LVI became more established, we incorporated client LVI results into the interviews to better understand the relationship between values and flourishing. Over time, our interviews expanded beyond life transitions and included working with clients on a wide range of clinical and performance issues. They also included a better understanding of organizational development through a lens of values-centered leadership.

Interviews were analyzed each year using systematic thematic analysis and synthesis (Boyatzis, 1998; Braun & Clark, 2006; Coffey & Atkinson, 1996; Crabtree, 1999; Creswell, 1994; Guest, 2012; Miles, 1994). After five years using this method of analysis, a pattern of themes emerged that distinguished effectiveness as it pertained to values and flourishing. It became clear that there was a dynamic relationship between values and fear; that perfectionism and procrastination were common ways of managing values-based fear; that management of values was as important as values clarification; that a chronically evaluative mindset was a frequent factor that negatively impacted resilience and effectiveness; and that authenticity, integrity, resilience, and striving for excellence were frequent intentional factors when people flourished. For the next 12 years, we infused these themes into the interviews to learn more about the nuances of what moved someone to a deeper level of effectiveness and what blocked it, while still keeping the interviews open-ended enough to learn other important contributing factors. During this phase of research, we particularly narrowed our focus to the factors of authenticity, integrity, resilience, and excellence (Csikszentmihalyi, 1990). Clients proved more likely to flourish when they could know and act on their own sense of authenticity, consistently align their values to their behavior, more confidently manage the hardness and harshness of the world around them, and focus their efforts on factors that contribute to excellence. As we explored these four factors with clients over those 12 years, the concepts presented in this book emerged.

Because our work was done with clients in clinical, academic, and work settings, the primary consideration was providing effective therapeutic counseling or consultation. The interviews' secondary consideration was to help individuals and organizations become more effective. So, as these concepts emerged, we were equally interested in how they could be developed and internalized for our clients. One of the most noteworthy findings from our work was the ongoing intentionality that is a part of flourishing. When our clients flourished, there was a consistent pattern of intentionality. They were actively mindful of the factors that led to flourishing because the noise of the world would drift them away from it. We clarified that mindset matters, but because the world continually pulls us from that mindset, we have to be intentional. As we began to see progress with the teaching and counseling of the strategies that fostered flourishing, the development of a distilled mental training program emerged, the Authentic Excellence Initiative, which incorporated the Five Paradigm Shifts that attended to the four factors of authenticity, integrity, resilience, and excellence (Crace, 2017; Crace & Lickerman, 2014).

The assessment of the Authentic Excellence Initiative has been positive and affirming (Crace, 2017). Evaluations indicated the following learning outcomes:

- Better understanding of the values that guide my behavior (4.45/5).
- Better understanding of how my values cause fulfillment and stress (4.41/5).
- Have clarified how to better align my values with my behavior (4.33/5).
- Better understanding of how to manage my values (4.26/5)
- Overall Evaluation (4.36/5).

At William & Mary, the Authentic Excellence Initiative reflected an integration of the organizational restructuring of our university's Division of Student Affairs with the principles of positive psychology and flourishing (Ambler, Crace, & Fisler, 2015; Fisler, Ambler, & Crace; 2014; Fredrickson, 2009; Keyes & Haidt, 2003; Lopez, 2008; Lopez & Snyder, 2011; Schreiner, 2015; Seligman, 2011; Seligman & Csikszentmihalyi, 2000; Williams, Horrell, Edmiston, & Brady, 2018). This culminated in the development of an integrative wellness center, which houses the Center for Mindfulness and Authentic Excellence (CMAX), a training/learning center for the research and practice of values-centered effectiveness. Over 2,000 students a year voluntarily participate in the Authentic Excellence training.

Our work continues to be refined and informed by the brilliant work of our colleagues in the areas of values development, values-centered leadership, life transition, positive psychology, performance psychology, neuroplasticity, wellness, and acceptance-based therapies (Almeida & Tavares, 2008; Brown, 1995; Cheng & Fleischmann, 2010; Clemens & Milsom, 2008; David, 2016; Ercegovac & Koludrovic, 2012; Fredrickson, 2009; Gentile, 2010; Greenberg, 2017; Hayes, Follette, & Linehan, 2004; Hayes & Smith, 2005; Kabat-Zinn, 1990; Keyes & Haidt, 2003; Lehrer, Woolfolk, & Sime; 2008; Linehan, 2014; Lopez, 2008; Lopez & Snyder, 2011; Meichenbaum, 1985; Mitchell, 1986; Salkind, 2007; Schreiner, 2015; Seligman, 2011; Seligman & Csikszentmihalyi, 2000; Song, Li, & Li, 2009; Subramanian, 2001; Subramanian & Kruthika, 2012; VanderWeele, McNeely, & Koh, 2019; Williams, Horrell, Edmiston, & Brady, 2018). This book is linked most notably to Mary Gentile's work on Giving Voice to Values (GVV) which provides a seminal foundation for the Authentic Excellence Initiative. GVV clearly demonstrates the importance and vitality of living our values, while respecting the difficulty of doing so. GVV asks the question, "Once you know the right thing to do, how do you get it done effectively?" This emphasis on action and effectiveness corresponds with the flourishing techniques of Authentic Excellence. Our program looks to improve functionality by training individuals to develop a relationship with how their values look in action. We then strategize how that individual can utilize a healthy relationship with their values to flourish in the context of their daily life. The individualized approach of flourishing that Authentic

Excellence teaches corresponds with GVV's Seven Pillars for effective values-driven behavior (Gentile, 2010).

Giving Voice to Values provides an empowering framework for effectively acting on moral values. The principles of the Authentic Excellence program complement GVV to embolden individuals to act on their values more than their fears, and to manage their values in a healthy manner. Throughout this book, when we refer to values, we are referring to personal values, which are both the basic beliefs that guide one's behavior, motivation, and decision-making, and also the lens through which we evaluate others and ourselves. All healthy personal values have a social context and, therefore, a certain level of societal "should" or moral weight associated with them. The reason for our focus on personal values has to do with the process of clarifying one's authenticity through a values lens.

To truly own a personal set of values, it requires time for challenging reflection in order to understand the influences that have shaped one's values and to clarify the values that will serve as a compass for one's behavior. During our empirical research on values assessment, moral values and virtues that had an obvious social weight (e.g., being honest) did very little to distinguish among individuals because everyone endorsed those values as high, whether they were acting on them or not. Values assessments are vulnerable to being only a picture of values that have the most positive social weight instead of a true glimpse into what matters to a person at the time of assessment. The higher moral weight a value has, the less likely one is to truly disclose whether they are really acting on that value. With the LVI, the fourteen values that were deemed the most stable empirically were values that had positive social weight but also had some variability as to how they were endorsed when relating values to behavior. We were interested in connecting individuals' values to their behavior and motivation when determining what mattered to them, not just reminding them of societal "shoulds".

For values assessment to play a role in flourishing and resilience, one must understand the past influences that shaped one's early values, to begin the process, during young adulthood, of shifting from values that one was raised with to internalizing one's own values, and to then develop a relational perspective with those values through active expression and management. As a person develops their personal set of values, they will also notice how those values intersect with those around them. They will find that others affirm some of their values in certain environments, and others dismiss or oppose some of their values in certain environments. We believe that if a person can accurately assess what truly matters to them at various times in their life and discern how those values can be healthfully expressed and managed in their behavior, then they are better equipped to understand and manage the relationship between their personal values and societally weighted moral values. Our efforts aim to help young adults secure a foundation of resilience for that difficult, but meaningful, work.

Your training

Throughout the book we provide sections for participation through periodic reflections and exercises to help you internalize the concepts. Participatory components can prevent the trend of "noble avoidance". The quests for self-awareness and self-improvement have become important threads in our culture. People are continuously seeking answers as to why they behave or feel the way they do. That's not a bad thing. But we've also noticed a trend of moving from book to book, video to video, podcast to podcast without devoting enough time to working on what was learned.

Making lasting change requires more than insight and learning. Insight is necessary for change, but insufficient. No amount of insight can replace or reduce the hard work necessary to reach a deeper level of excellence and fulfillment. Fortunately, that's not the problem we have found with most people. People can do hard. They just need to know where to direct their energies and to trust that the work will lead to something. Human beings will hold on to the most maladaptive patterns of behavior if they don't trust that there is something better. We encourage you to spend time with this book, do the reflective exercises, do the training, and give yourself time to live the principles.

Thank you for taking the time to better understand what your authentic excellence looks like and how to consistently maintain it. We appreciate your curiosity.

Key points

1. The relentless pace and uncertainty of our current world creates a life of ongoing and overlapping change.
2. For young adults, the combination of a relentless world and imposed portfolio culture creates a pressure where each step of advancement has incredible implications for future opportunities. Fear is now exceeding trust resulting in a plateau effect where young adults are vulnerable to staying "stuck at good".
3. This book explores the factors that cause a plateau effect and introduces a training process to optimize personal effectiveness defined as consistent levels of productivity, fulfillment, and resilience.

Personalizing the concepts

1. In this world of constant change, what transition or important change are you currently managing?
2. Because we are impacted by those around us, what transitions and important changes are others close to you currently experiencing?
3. What specific uncertainty is most prominent in your life right now? How are you experiencing that uncertainty emotionally and mentally? How are you managing that uncertainty?

For younger teens and professionals who work with young adults

The concepts in this book are targeted toward young adults, aged 17–29, but can also be useful for younger teens and for individuals who work with, mentor, or supervise young adults.

For younger teens: As you read through the book, pick one or two concepts from Part I that speak to you and feel relevant for this time in your life. For Part II, choose one Paradigm Shift that speaks to you and practice it for a few months before moving on to another Paradigm Shift.

For professionals who work with young adults: Read the book from a conversational lens. Rather than trying to master the material to teach, pick a few concepts that resonate for you and that can be incorporated into genuine conversations with young adults. How do these concepts get played out in their lives? Learn from them as they learn from you. Take a relational approach in the trust that conversational learning is often the deepest way to understand values. From that conversation, a goal or strategy from the book will emerge collaboratively that you can then mentor and support.

References

Almeida, L., & Tavares, P. (2008). Life Values Inventory: Studies with Portuguese college students. *International Journal of Psychology*, 43(3–4), 484.

Ambler, V.M., Crace, R.K., & Fisler, J. (2015). Nurturing genius: Positive psychology as a framework for organization and practice. *About Campus, 19,* 24–28.

Boyatzis, R. (1998). *Transforming qualitative information: Thematic analysis and code development*. Thousand Oaks, CA: Sage.

Braun, V. & Clarke, V. (2006). Using thematic analysis in psychology. *Qualitative Research in Psychology*, 3(2), 77–101.

Brown, D. (1995). A values-based approach to facilitating career transitions. *The Career Development Quarterly*, 44(1), 4–11.

Brown, D., & Crace, R.K. (1996a). *Life Values Inventory: Manual and user's guide*. Chapel Hill, NC: Life Values Resources.

Brown, D., & Crace, R.K. (1996b). *Life Values Inventory: Occupations locator*. Chapel Hill, NC: Life Values Resources.

Brown, D., & Crace, R.K. (1997a). *Life Values Inventory: Educational majors locator*. Chapel Hill, NC: Life Values Resources.

Brown, D., & Crace, R.K. (1997b). *Life Values Inventory: Leisure activities locator*. Chapel Hill, NC: Life Values Resources.

Brown, D., & Crace, R.K. (2002). *Facilitator's guide to the Life Values Inventory* (Revised ed.). Williamsburg, VA: Applied Psychology Resources.

Brown, D., Crace, R.K., & Almeida, L. (2006). A culturally sensitive, values-based approach to career counseling. In A.J. Palmo, W.J. Weikel, & D.P. Borsos (Eds.), *Foundations of mental health counseling* (3rd ed., pp. 144–171). Springfield, IL: Charles C. Thomas.

Cheng, A., & Fleischmann, K. (2010). Developing a meta-inventory of human values. *Proceedings of the Association for Information Science and Technology*, 47(1), 1–10.

Clemens, E., & Milsom, A. (2008). Enlisted service members' transition into the civilian world of work: A cognitive information processing approach. *The Career Development Quarterly*, 56(3), 246–256.

Coffey, A., & Atkinson, P. (1996). *Making sense of qualitative data*. Thousand Oaks, CA: Sage.

Crabtree, B. (1999). *Doing qualitative research*. Thousand Oaks, CA: Sage.

Crace, R.K. (1992). *The development of an instrument to empirically assess life values* (Doctoral dissertation). Retrieved from ProQuest Dissertations and Theses.

Crace, R.K. (2005, April). Organizational and team development consulting for academic and administrative departments. In J.J. Kandell (Chair), *Innovations in college counseling*. Symposium conducted at the annual meeting of the American College Personnel Association (ACPA), Nashville, TN.

Crace, R.K. (2007, February). *Optimal self-leadership and substance abuse education*. Keynote address at the annual meeting of the Virginia Tidewater Consortium for Higher Education's Leadership Conference on Alcohol, Other Drugs and Violence Prevention in Higher Education, Norfolk, VA.

Crace, R.K. (2008, January). *Optimal self-leadership principles for parents of high ability students*. Workshop presented at the annual meeting of the Center for Gifted Education Conference, Williamsburg, VA.

Crace, R.K. (2010a, February). *Values & resilience: Leading others to flourish*. Invited presentation at the annual meeting of the Atlantic Coast Conference Student Leadership Conference, Tallahassee, FL.

Crace, R.K. (2010b, November). *Values clarification and flourishing: It's not "what" but "how."* Concluding keynote address at the annual meeting of the North Carolina Career Development Association, Elon, NC.

Crace, R.K. (2011a, August). *Life values, college student transitions, and grief.* Keynote address at the annual meeting of the National Conference on College Student Grief, Raleigh, NC.

Crace, R.K. (2011b, September). *Emerging adults, values & flourishing*. Psychiatry Grand Rounds, Duke Hospital, Durham, NC.

Crace, R.K. (2012a, March). *Life Values Inventory Online*. In J.J. Kandell (Chair), Innovations in college counseling. Symposium presented at the annual meeting of the American College Personnel Association (ACPA), Louisville, KY.

Crace, R.K. (2012b, August). *Cultivating wisdom during the grieving process*. Keynote address at the annual meeting of the National Conference on College Student Grief, Raleigh, NC.

Crace, R.K. (2013a, March). *Emerging adulthood: The pursuit of excellence or calm?* Pediatrics Grand Rounds, Duke Hospital, Durham, NC.

Crace, R.K. (2013b, June). *Cultivating wisdom and integrity among our residents*. Featured presentation as invited expert-in-residence at the annual meeting of the American College & University Housing Organization-International (ACUHO-I), Minneapolis, MN.

Crace, R.K. (2013c, June). *Dynamic blueprinting for wellness and authentic excellence*. Featured presentation as invited expert-in-residence at the annual meeting of ACUHO-I, Minneapolis, MN.

Crace, R.K. (2017, July). *Resilience in a relentless world*. Workshop presented at the Fifth World Congress on Positive Psychology, International Positive Psychology Association, Montreal, Canada.

Crace, R.K., & Brown, D. (1996). *Understanding your values.* Chapel Hill, NC: Life Values Resources.

Crace, R.K., & Brown, D. (1997). *Life Values Inventory: User's guide.* Chapel Hill, NC: Life Values Resources.

Crace, R.K., & Brown, D. (2002a). *Life Values Inventory* (Revised ed.). Williamsburg, VA: Applied Psychology Resources.

Crace, R.K., & Brown, D. (2002b). *Understanding your values* (Revised ed.). Williamsburg, VA: Applied Psychology Resources.

Crace, R.K. & Brown, D. (2006). Life Values Inventory. In N.J. Salkind (Ed.), *Encyclopedia of measurement and statistics* (Vol. 2). Thousand Oaks, CA: Sage.

Crace, R.K., & Brown, D. (2012). *Life Values Inventory Online.* Durham, NC: Life Values Inventory Online, Inc. Available at www.lifevaluesinventory.org.

Crace, R.K., & Hardy, C.J. (1996). Sport psychology and the injured athlete. In E.J. Shahady (Ed.), *Primary care sports medicine* (pp. 669–680). Cambridge, MA: Blackwell Scientific.

Crace, R.K., & Hardy, C.J. (1997). Individual values and the team building process. *Journal of Applied Sport Psychology, 9*(1), 41–60.

Crace, R.K., & Ivy, R. (2011, August). *Grief and community resource coordination: When students need additional support.* Presentation at the annual meeting of the National Conference on College Student Grief, Raleigh, NC.

Crace, R.K., & Lickerman, A. (2014, June). *An upstream approach to suicide prevention: Promoting resilience in college students.* Presentation at the meeting of the SAMHSA Garrett Lee Smith Suicide Prevention Grantee Conference, Washington, DC.

Creswell, J. (1994). *Research design: Qualitative & quantitative approaches.* Thousand Oaks, CA: Sage.

Csikszentmihalyi, M. (1990). *Flow: The psychology of optimal experience* (1st ed.). New York: Harper & Row.

David, S. (2016). *Emotional agility: Get unstuck, embrace change, and thrive in work and life.* New York: Avery.

Ercegovac, I., & Koludrovic, M. (2012). Life values and divorce: Intergeneration and family perspective. *Sociology and Space, 50*(2), 257–273.

Fisler, J., Ambler, V.M., & Crace, R.K. (2014, March). *Positive psychology as a framework for student affairs practice.* Presentation at the annual meeting of the National Association for Student Personnel Administrators (NASPA), Baltimore, MD.

Fredrickson, B. L. (2009). *Positivity.* New York: Crown.

Gentile, M.C. (2010). *Giving voice to values: How to speak your mind when you know what's right.* New Haven, CT: Yale University Press.

Greenberg, M. (2017). *The stress-proof brain: Master your emotional response to stress using mindfulness & neuroplasticity.* Oakland, CA: New Harbinger.

Guest, G. (2012). *Applied thematic analysis.* Thousand Oaks, CA: Sage.

Hardy, C.J., Burke, K.L., & Crace, R.K. (2005). Coaching: An effective communication system. In S. Murphy (Ed.), *The sport psych handbook: A complete guide to today's best mental training techniques* (pp. 191–212). Champaign, IL: Human Kinetics.

Hardy, C.J., & Crace, R.K. (1991). The effects of task structure and teammate competence on social loafing. *Journal of Sport and Exercise Psychology, 13,* 372–381.

Hardy, C.J., & Crace, R.K. (1993). The dimensions of social support when dealing with sport injuries. In D. Pargman (Ed.), *Psychological bases of sport injuries* (pp. 121–144). Morgantown, WV: Fitness Information Technology.

Hardy, C.J., & Crace, R.K. (1997). Foundations of team building: Introduction to the team building primer. *Journal of Applied Sport Psychology*, 9(1), 1–10.

Hardy, C.J., Crace, R.K., & Burke, K.L. (1999). Social support and injury: A framework for social support-based interventions with injured athletes. In D. Pargman (Ed.), *Psychological bases of sport injuries* (2nd ed., pp. 175–198). Morgantown, WV: Fitness Information Technology.

Hayes, S.C., Follette, V.M., & Linehan, M.M. (Eds.) (2004). *Mindfulness and acceptance: Expanding the cognitive-behavioral tradition.* New York: Guilford.

Hayes, S.C., & Smith, S. (2005). *Get out of your mind and into your life: The new acceptance and commitment therapy.* Oakland, CA: New Harbinger.

Kabat-Zinn, J. (1990). *Full catastrophe living: Using the wisdom of your body and mind to face stress, pain and illness.* New York: Delacorte.

Keyes, C.L.M., & Haidt, J. (Eds.) (2003). *Flourishing: Positive psychology and the life well lived.* Washington, DC: American Psychological Association.

Lehrer, P.M., Woolfolk, R.L., & Sime, W.E. (Eds.) (2008). *Principles and practice of stress management* (3rd ed.). New York: Guilford.

Linehan, M.M. (2014). *DBT skills training manual* (2nd ed.). New York: Guilford.

Lopez, S.J. (Ed.). (2008). *Positive psychology: Exploring the best in people* (Vols. 1–4). Westport, CT: Praeger.

Lopez, S.J., & Snyder, C.R. (Eds.). (2011). *Oxford handbook of positive psychology.* Oxford: Oxford University Press.

Meichenbaum, D. (1985). *Stress inoculation training.* New York: Prentice-Hall.

Meilman, P.W., Crace, R.K., Presley, C.A., Lyerla, R. (1995). Beyond performance enhancement: Polypharmacy among collegiate users of steroids. *Journal of American College Health*, 44, 98–104.

Miles, M.B. (1994). *Qualitative data analysis: An expanded sourcebook.* Thousand Oaks, CA: Sage.

Mitchell, J.V. (1986). Relationships between attitudes toward higher education and life values. *Assessment and Evaluation in Higher Education*, 11(2), 93–104.

Salkind, N.J. (2007). Quality of Well-Being Scale. *Encyclopedia of Measurement and Statistics* (pp. 532–533). Thousand Oaks, CA: Sage.

Schreiner, L.A. (2015). Positive psychology and higher education. In J.C. Wader, L.I. Marks, & R.D. Hetzel (Eds.), *Positive psychology on the college campus* (pp. 1–25). New York: Oxford University.

Seligman, M.E.P. (2011). *Flourish: A visionary new understanding of happiness and well-being.* New York: Free Press.

Seligman, M.E.P., & Csikszentmihalyi, M. (2000). Positive psychology: An introduction. *American Psychologist*, 55(1), 5–14.

Silva, J.M., & Crace, R.K. (1987). *Psychological assessment of the United States men's national Team Handball team.* Technical report made to The United States Team Handball Federation (400 pp.), Colorado Springs, CO.

Silva, J.M., Hardy, C.J., & Crace, R.K. (1988). Analysis of psychological momentum in intercollegiate tennis. *Journal of Sport and Exercise Psychology*, 10, 346–354.

Song, L., Li, X., & Li R. (2009). An empirical research of life values of the Chinese post-80s youngsters. *Qingdao Daxue Shifanxueyuan Xuebao (Journal of Teachers College Qingdao University)*, 26(2), 21–27.

Subramanian, S. (2001). Life values and perceived occupational stress among cosmopolitan (scientific) and local (administrative)-oriented scientists in R & D organizations. *Asia Pacific Business Review*, 6(4), 74–81.

Subramanian, S., & Kruthika, J. (2012). Psychological factors determining high intentions to join defence services among adolescents. *Journal of Organisation and Human Behaviour*, 1(2), 39–45.

VanderWeele, T., McNeely, E., & Koh, H. (2019, April 1). Reimagining health—flourishing. *Journal of the American Medical Association (JAMA)*. doi: 10.1001/jama.2019.3035.

Williams, N., Horrell, L., Edmiston, D., & Brady, M. (2018). The impact of positive psychology on higher education. *The William & Mary Educational Review*, 5(1), 83–94.

Notes

2 Values

The ironic precursor to the plateau effect

At the age of 25, Sean had the opportunity to transition from temp work to an entry-level position at a rising insurance firm. After three years, he was offered a leadership position in the company that would involve supervising a small department of a dozen young professionals. He relished the opportunity but was anxious. His shyness and humility had established a pattern of followership. Sean had shied away from leadership opportunities in the past but loved developing mentoring relationships where he learned about values-centered philosophies.

During the first month in his new position, Sean took his group on a retreat to develop a values and vision statement that was congruent with the mission statement of the company. He met with members of his team and learned what was important to them professionally and personally. The retreat set an effective tone as Sean's colleagues seemed to enjoy their work and responded to him well as a leader.

A few months later, Sean noticed a difference in how the team was functioning. Nothing was wrong per se, but the tone had shifted in the office. It felt like a collection of individual silos instead of a team. Some members were controlling, and others procrastinated until deadlines demanded action. In individual conversations with his team, there seemed to be a lot of judgment toward each other that was resulting in small resentments and frustrations. Despite these subtle issues, the team was being productive toward their goals, but not at the level he knew they could be. Sean internalized this shift as some flaw in his leadership. What was he doing wrong? Why were these good people behaving in ways that affected their performance, and how could he turn it around?

In today's world, a lot of attention is devoted to values and their importance for success. Organizations devote significant time to developing their mission, values, and vision statements in the belief that effectively communicating these statements will lead to enhanced planning and performance. Similarly, professionals in human development and leadership espouse the importance of values clarification for motivation, purpose, decision-making, and social change. Knowing your "why" before clarifying the "what" and "how" has become a new mantra. And for good reason, values do matter, especially in the context of flourishing and resilience.

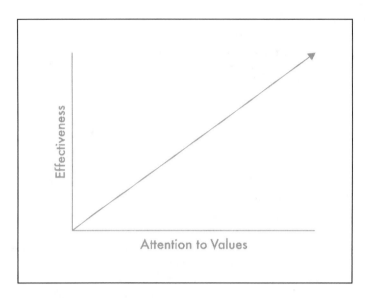

Figure 2.1 Perceived effectiveness

Most have described the relationship between values and effectiveness as a positive, linear relationship. In other words, there is an assumption that the more attention we give to our values, the more effective we will be, as depicted in Figure 2.1.

It makes sense. The linear relationship is founded on the reasonable assumption that if we clarify what's important to us, then we tap into a deep level of motivation that will lead to more purposeful and direct action (see Figure 2.2). Not only that, but there is a belief that if we focus and direct our energies toward what really matters to us, then everything should work out fine.

Unfortunately, we have found that it's not quite that simple or linear. Instead, attention to values resembles more of a curvilinear relationship to effectiveness, as seen in Figure 2.3. It is true that to have any chance of flourishing, we must devote some attention and energy to our values. But there is a point of diminishing return that requires intentional management strategies to move beyond.

The moment we clarify our values and commit to them, we find ourselves frequently experiencing conflicting motivations and conflicting actions (see Figure 2.4). We are vulnerable to a cascade of *"what if's"* that can impact our motivation, decisions, and actions. *"What if I fail? What if I'm rejected or hurt? What if this affects my future? What if others evaluate me negatively? What if others in power see me unfairly? What if I am in an environment where I'm being marginalized? What if I'm trying to decide between two competing*

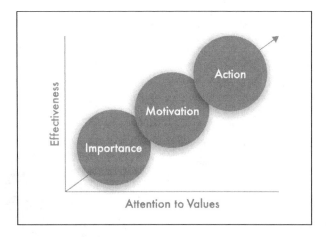

Figure 2.2 Perceived motivations and actions

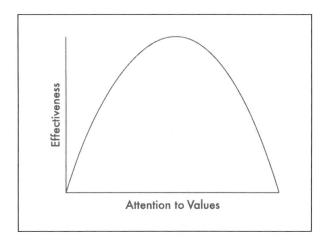

Figure 2.3 Curvilinear effectiveness

values; which value is most right for this situation? What if I make a decision now that I will regret in the future and then feel trapped?" **Essentially, if you care about something, stakes become involved. So when we commit our energies to our values, we encounter certain vulnerabilities that we don't naturally manage very well.**

As in the case of Sean in the example, we often find that organizational leaders experience a plateau with their team after genuinely trying to lead with the group's values. Leaders often attribute the plateau to something they

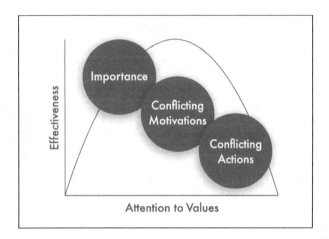

Figure 2.4 Conflicting motivations and actions

must be doing wrong. Individuals who strive for values-centered living also describe this experience and conclusion. They had bought into the "live your passion, live your values" message and were finding themselves stuck.

Why does values-centered living get in our way? Chapter 3 explores the plateau effect.

Key points

1. The relationship between values and effectiveness resembles more of a curvilinear relationship than a linear progression.
2. While values-centered living is crucial for flourishing and resilience, it also creates vulnerabilities that we are not naturally good at managing. If not properly managed, these vulnerabilities can interfere with our effectiveness.

Personalizing the concepts

1. Think of a couple of values that are important to you. What do those values look like in action during your everyday life?
2. What do those values in action look like when they are most effective?
3. What do they look like when they are not as effective? What's getting in the way?

Notes

3 Stuck at good

The plateau effect

Joanna and Toni were at the top of their high school class. Toni envied Joanna's ability to leave her studies until the last minute and still pull off high grades. It became a source of pride and distinction for Joanna. She could spend the day doing whatever she wanted and then take care of her work at the last minute. During those rare times when Joanna would begin an assignment early, she would exhaust herself with perfectionism. It was overwhelming. So, she quickly learned that if she waited until something had to be done, she would be motivated and focused.

Conversely, Joanna admired how Toni could devote herself to her studies and work hard without getting overwhelmed. Toni would start a project as soon as it was assigned and work until she had mastered the assignment. Toni took pride in her mantra, "You may be smarter than me, but you'll never outwork me."

Now at different colleges, Joanna and Toni had just received their midterm grades and, for the first time in their academic careers, both had three Cs.

For Joanna, the beginning of college had gone so well. She'd formed great friendships with the women of her hall, and she and her roommate had pledged for the same sorority. She actually felt more connected at college than at high school. However, the professors were a little intense, and assigned amounts of reading that were ridiculous. Her standard cram routine wasn't working. She studied materials a, b, and c, but the professors were asking about materials f, t, and x based on an understanding of a, b, and c. Joanna knew she was going to have to work much harder. But what if she lost close friends for the sake of working harder on subjects she didn't even like?

Toni enjoyed spending time with the women of her hall during Orientation and for the first week of classes. But she was soon looking at 300 pages of reading a night, two papers a week, and lab projects. She began to feel overwhelmed and started to fall behind. "Just outwork everyone," she told herself. So, Toni reduced her sleep to four hours a night, spent most of her time in the library, stopped going to the gym, and cut off contact with her friends. She believed the sacrifices would pay off.

Toni knew she hadn't done as well on her midterms as she had hoped, but three Cs? She knew the material but when the time came to perform during *testing, she choked. She was so anxious she could barely breathe, much less think clearly. Toni had never been so anxious, upset, or miserable in her life.*

Both Joanna and Toni knew a change was necessary but were unsure how to reconstruct behaviors that had served them so well.

Why do certain natural patterns of managing fear and pressure level off in terms of effectiveness and wellbeing? Is it due to a lack of self-discipline, motivation, or willpower? No; being vulnerable to the plateau of effectiveness and wellbeing is the result of caring. It is essentially what happens when we confirm that something or someone has become important.

Once you care about something or someone, there are **three unavoidable truths** that cannot be escaped:

1. **Uncertainty**. You never completely control everything that goes into what is important. There is always a chance you may fail or lose what is important to you.
2. **Cost**. If you were to fail or lose what was important, there would be a personal cost and you would be hurt in some manner.
3. **Perceived evaluation**. When you engage in what's important, you are also aware that opinions are being formed about you. You recognize that you and others are evaluating your actions. Furthermore, your perceptions of how you are being evaluated are not always accurate.

The "What if" moment

Because of these three unavoidable truths, whenever you engage in something that matters, you become aware of "What if?". *"What if I fail at or lose this object of importance?"* This evokes a natural **fear of failure**. It's not a fear that feels the same as danger, but it is an unsettling emotion that is tied to the awareness of caring about something that is uncertain and potentially costly. We tend to experience fear of failure in the form of **pressure**.

Once you experience this pressure, your natural tendency to manage fear of failure is to drift toward two coping patterns: (1) **over-control/mastery—** aka **perfectionism**, or (2) **avoidance/escape until it "has to" be attended to**—aka **procrastination**.

Perfectionism (over-control) and procrastination (avoidance) are the most natural ways to manage the fear associated with caring. If I can engage in something I care about as perfectly as possible, then I don't have to worry about failure. Alternatively, if I can distance myself from the discomfort of fear, then I don't have to worry about failure until I'm forced to engage in something I care about. By the time I'm forced to act, I'll be so focused on the immediacy of the situation that there won't be much room for fear or worry.

Figure 3.1 is a depiction of what we call the **Fear-Based Model of Excellence**. It's an approach that actually leads to temporary excellence. Perfectionism creates a drive that can lead to high levels of preparation and performance. In

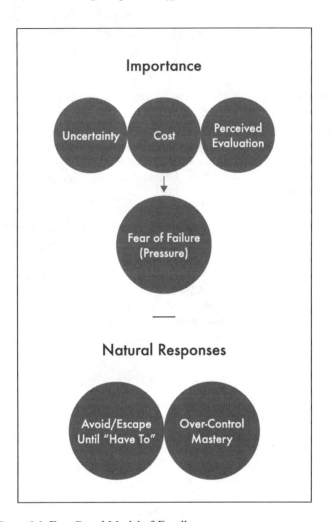

Figure 3.1 Fear-Based Model of Excellence

terms of procrastination, if one is talented enough, there is something neuro-logically natural about distancing oneself from discomfort and then allowing the stress of the "have to" moment to engage one's crisis system. There can even be a sense of pride in being able to pull things off at the last minute. Ironically, procrastination can even help us contain our perfectionism. If I have perfectionistic tendencies and ten hours in which to do a project, I will be prone to spending most of the ten hours working on the project to make sure it's done as perfectly as possible. But if part of me doesn't want to work on the project for ten hours, then procrastination allows me to shrink that work to a two-hour "have to" timeframe.

Unfortunately, along with the positive benefits of perfectionism and pro-crastination, there are costs. Managing pressure through over-control and avoidance jumpstarts the nervous system into action and that can tax us phys-ically and psychologically.

Think of these coping patterns within the context of intensity, relief, and emotional residue. Perfectionism is characterized by long bouts of intensity with short periods of relief and the emotional residue is chronic worry and frustration. The intensity comes from the mixture of drive and fear. The worry comes from uncertainty and the frustration that we don't control everything in the way we want or need to. From a strictly performance and effectiveness perspective, perfectionism gets in the way because we are **pressing** too hard. When this happens, a value, a belief that guides our behavior and filters how we see ourselves and others, is drifting to a **need**. There is a huge difference between the need to belong and the value of Belonging, or between the need to achieve and the value of Achieving. Unchecked, this coping pattern can fuel anxiety and anxiety-based depression.

Conversely, procrastination is characterized by long bouts of relief with short periods of intensity and the emotional residue is guilt. While there may be some pride in being able to pull off last-minute results, you never fully escape the guilt of avoidance or the worry that you will not be able to con-tinually do so effectively. In addition, avoidance can start to become a gen-eral response to any emotional discomfort. That's the behavior that is often viewed by others as laziness. People who look lazy are often highly motivated but they are motivated to avoid. People who appear lazy can devote a lot of energy to experiencing the protective comfort of avoidance. They learned the effectiveness of avoidance when facing high-pressure challenges and now apply that methodology to any challenge they encounter.

The problem with procrastination is that we start relying on **hope** rather than on hard work. In our disengagement, we find ourselves hoping that "*the test won't be too hard*"; "*our supervisor will be in a good mood*"; "*our closest relationships won't force us to take risks*". Hope is a wonderful thing, but not as a motivational strategy. When we start relying on hope and find ourselves in a pattern of avoidance, a value is drifting into a **want**. We're treating a value like a preference. We have many preferences and wants in our lives, but preferences don't carry consistent motivational drive. When something that is important to us does not consistently show in our actions, we are vulnerable to judging ourselves. Unchecked, this pattern can move from guilt to shame and depression.

So, while this fear-based model can lead to excellence, **it unfortunately creates a ceiling effect and an increasing cost over time.** Perfectionism and pro-crastination eventually stop being optimally effective. When that occurs, if we don't have another way of managing our fear, we often resort to caring less in order to reduce the fear. It switches from the pursuit of excellence to the pursuit of calm.

The Fear-Based Model of Excellence explains our natural way of coping with pressure. It is not an awful thing and it typically just keeps us stuck at good. If we become too entrenched in these coping patterns, it can negatively impact our health and effectiveness considerably. However, these patterns of managing values-based fear are fully human and natural.

Fear of failure across generations

Every generation has its cultural legacy of hardship, tragedy, uncertainty, beauty, and success. Values and fear play an important role in the decision-making and actions of a culture. Many emerging adults of this generation have a higher incidence of fear of failure than previous generations because of something wise and wonderful about them. They no longer want to be successful; they want to be successful in something meaningful. However, the competition for those meaningful opportunities has never been more fierce. The awareness of importance and meaning is higher, uncertainty is higher and, as a result, fear is higher. So by the time many emerging adults reach college age, they have become specialists in perfectionism and procrastination by attaining success with these coping patterns. But it's during these years (for some earlier and some later) when young adults can begin to experience the ceiling effect and the costs of fear-based models of coping.

Other generations' relationship to fear and values can influence young adults. For instance, many parents of this generation are aware of the competitive pressures their children face. Oftentimes, they want their children to succeed and they want to play a part in that success. If parents see obstacles or their children drifting from a path of success, fear is triggered. From that place of fear, some parents can be prone to over-controlling their children and the challenges around them. As a result, the children of such parents can learn to become passive because through their avoidance they know their parents will often step in. This example of parental influence originated with a parent's care and concern, but when uncertainty and potential costs developed on their children's path, fear started to lead the parent's actions. When fear leads, we slip into our natural pattern of over-control or avoidance.

Furthermore, in some families the influence of extended family members is an important part of development. Older generations' relationship to fear and values affect how they interpret the challenges of younger generations. For instance, older generations that experienced large-scale war and depression grew up in a culture where introspection and reflection were seen as potentially dangerous and threatening. "Doing what was thought to be right" and giving little thought to how one felt became a common theme among these generations. There was a collectivism around values, and communities held on to those values as a form of survival. In response to racial bias and systemic trauma, a number of people in marginalized communities formed cultural sets of values and methods of coping. In both privileged and oppressed communities, many believed that one couldn't survive alone against threat and fear; it required a community. Therefore, individual feelings and motivations were often viewed as secondary. Conversely, many from the Baby Boom generation countered previous generations by encouraging introspection and honoring individual feelings, sometimes to the point of self-centered extremes. Generational components of extended family members can inspire but also discourage young adults, causing tension in familial relationships. For example, older grandparents may not understand striving for what makes one feel happy, or struggling to find motivation to act on things that seem easy to "just do".

Explaining the plateau effect

We've learned that the moment we dare to care, it makes us vulnerable to fear of failure, which human beings don't typically manage well. We naturally turn to perfectionism, procrastination, or both. Consequently, there is an increasing cost and a ceiling effect that occurs from this pattern of coping.

But why specifically does this create a plateau effect?

Whenever you lead with fear, you drift from a focus on your values—what's important to you—to a place of **need**. When afraid, you need reassurance that everything is going to be okay. You satisfy that need by becoming very dependent on **outcomes** and comparisons. As long as you have outcomes like grades, achievements, positive evaluations, and affirmations from others, you can start to have confidence that you'll be okay. But the more you become dependent on outcomes, the more you start to keep score. You start **evaluating** how things are going (see Figure 3.2).

The reason this causes us to plateau is because it creates a **chronically evaluative mindset**. Your brain never fully shuts off from the question, "How am I doing now?" and more specifically, "How am I doing relative to others?" You fall into a never-ending cycle of compensatory need and evaluation. On days when you don't experience outcomes to reassure you, your fear increases, which increases your need for outcomes to make up for this bad day. This constant cycle of needing outcomes and evaluating yourself at the end of every day eventually leads to chronic worry, intensity, and guilt. The cycle affects critical and creative thinking as well as satisfaction and wellbeing. It makes us too dependent and sensitive to factors that we don't control. We can become highly comparative to others often to the point where we start to avoid or care less.

Terry agreed to work through the weekend again. He was the only copywriter in the ad agency whose name the Creative Directors were starting to remember. "I'll make it through these project deadlines then ask for a raise."

Terry got the raise and immediately promised himself, "I've got to come in an hour earlier and make sure I stay later than everybody else."

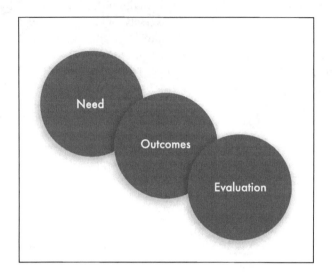

Figure 3.2 The plateau effect

Over the course of a year Terry became a fixture in the creative department, and was regularly assigned important accounts. However, his bosses seemed to be crossing the line from rewarding Terry's hard work to taking advantage of his work ethic. "Just keep hanging in there and they will make you Creative Director," he assured himself.

Terry was offered a Creative Director position after five years at the agency. "How am I going to pull off all these accounts with all these people under me?"

Terry started to feel more insecure in his abilities when he saw the work other Creative Directors were producing. His anxiety and stress levels were overwhelming and agency executives were beginning to notice. Terry tried to calm himself: "If I just keep plowing through, they'll eventually make me partner."

Mainly because of client insistence, the ad agency reluctantly made Terry partner. "How am I going to win over the other partners? How can I prove my gratitude to the clients that supported me?"

After ten years, Terry left the advertising agency. The relief was tremendous but short-lived when he decided to join his brother in an opportunity to open a restaurant. The business was successful, but every time Terry doubled-checked the impressive monthly figures, he would strategize, "How can we make a second or third location stand out in this market?"

There is another unintended and sad consequence of this cycle. As we "need" to chase outcomes, we experience less joy when we actually attain those outcomes. **When we are in a "need" state, the first emotion we experience once we attain an outcome is relief, not joy.** From that relief, we'll take a deep breath and soon fix our attention on the next outcome. This only serves to amplify our self-comparison to others and constant judgment.

How do transitions amplify the plateau effect?

If all change has some loss and uncertainty attached to it, the natural desire to avoid or over-control is intensified. During life transitions, we tend to rely on outcomes to inform us whether we've made the right decision or not. However, by the time we can evaluate what the outcomes are telling us, another challenge or change often comes along before we are settled. In periods of constant change, such as the life transitions young adults face, we encounter amplified uncertainty and loss. Our natural coping patterns of over-control and avoidance can become more entrenched during periods of change, which can lead to regular plateau effects.

Key points

1. When we clarify that something is important to us, there are three unavoidable truths that we cannot escape: uncertainty, potential cost, and perceived evaluation from others.
2. These three unavoidable consequences of care evoke a natural fear of failure. Once we experience this pressure, our natural tendency to manage fear of failure is through over-control (perfectionism) and/or avoidance (procrastination).
3. While the Fear-Based Model of Excellence explains our natural way of coping with fear of failure, it unfortunately creates a ceiling effect and an increasing cost over time. It's what keeps us stuck at good.
4. Many young adults experience high levels of pressure because of their strong desire to engage in a career that has meaning to them, but the competition for those meaningful opportunities is extremely fierce. This competitive atmosphere instills more fear than trust. Therefore, young adults can become reliant on perfectionism and procrastination as a means to manage that fear.
5. The plateau effect occurs because when we lead with fear, we look for reassurance that everything is going to be okay. We do so by becoming overly dependent on outcomes. This results in a chronically evaluative and comparative mindset that disrupts our effectiveness.

Personalizing the concepts

1. When do you feel pressure stemming from a fear of failure? When are you prone to cope through over-control? When are you prone to cope through avoidance?
2. What messages did you hear from others growing up about fear? Among your family, peers, teachers, and coaches, how was fear discussed and

described, if at all? How did those messages influence how you currently manage fear?

3. What are the benefits of the patterns you use to manage fear and what are the costs? How have you experienced a ceiling effect with how you manage fear?

4. Describe a transition in your life where uncertainty and/or loss was challenging. What were the coping patterns that helped you adjust, and what would you do differently to better manage the fears associated with that transition?

Notes

4 Secondary vulnerabilities of fear-based excellence

Aaron had been preparing for the Olympic Trials for seven years. At the age of 21 he finally qualified, throwing his PR (Personal Record) in the men's discus at the College Conference Finals. When Aaron was 14, his high school coach, a former discus thrower, had suggested he consider the event. Aaron was a natural. He dedicated himself in practice and expounded upon the advanced expertise of his coach. He fell in love with the complexity of the discus throw by studying the biomechanics of the movement. In one throw, there was power, grace, tension, looseness, balance, leverage, and force. His success in the sport quickly became his identity. He won the State Championship in his sophomore year and continued to improve throughout high school. He had his pick of colleges on scholarship and chose the school that had the best Field program. People had mentioned the Olympics for the past few years and now it was close to becoming a reality.

While traveling to the Trials, Aaron was relaxed, feeling he had earned the opportunity through sacrifice and hard work. But he wasn't the only one who had made sacrifices. His family and coaches had invested a lot of time, energy, and money into his dream.

The morning of the Trials he couldn't stop thinking, "What if I don't qualify for the Olympics? What if others deserve it more? What if I fail?" Aaron needed to qualify to prove to everyone who had believed in him that their sacrifices were worth it. He needed to qualify to pave the way for his future. He knew medaling was an unrealistic expectation, but "Olympian" was the title he needed to get into grad school, to get the job he wanted, to connect with people of stature and respect. No one could ever take that title away from him… but what if?

First throw… scratch… second throw… muscled it… last throw—"Oh s**t, last throw. Come on, you deserve this."

We have explained how values-based fear can lead to a plateau effect if not managed effectively. However, it also can lead to other vulnerabilities that we don't naturally manage well.

The need for equity and fairness

Fear of failure creates a need for outcomes to reassure us that we're going to be okay and that our efforts were worth the trouble. Unfortunately, this also creates a need for equity and fairness. "I studied for the test, so I want a return on my investment." Outcomes require alignment with forces outside our control. So if we need outcomes, then we need the world to cooperate in order to be reassured, which can put us in a vulnerable state. We all prefer and hope for fairness, but when we need outcomes, the demand for equity and fairness becomes critical. And when we don't receive equity we can become highly resentful of the world around us, or over-personalize the inequities as a statement of our inability. If we are resentful, it can unintentionally cause us to drift to a place of entitlement. If we over-personalize, we can develop hampering insecurities.

Guilt and judgment

"I can't believe I let another week go by without painting." Amy had promised herself that she wouldn't give up on her art when she took a new management position. Waiting tables after college provided a good balance of art and paying bills. She could paint during the day, work at night, and when she clocked out, work didn't come home with her.

Amy was a hard worker and great with people. Eventually, she got the best shifts and her bosses began to take notice of her work ethic. Her job coupled with a healthy personal life of friends and relationships limited her time to paint, but she was still able to get to the canvas a decent amount each week. When the owners of the restaurant opened a new establishment at another location, Amy was their first choice to manage the place. She knew this step would mean less time for herself, her relationships, and her painting, but she wanted the consistent paycheck, and a management position at a popular restaurant could lead to own-ership and consulting opportunities. "Think of all the painting I could get done as an owner."

Six years later, Amy was a small percentage owner and General Manager at a very busy downtown restaurant. Her work schedule was overwhelming. There was pressure to establish her voice among the investors, and she was responsible for a large staff of people who depended on her. One of the most meaningful facets of her life, painting, had been routinely losing out to other priorities that seemed to have a momentum of their own.

On New Year's Day, she vowed to commit one hour a day to painting. She had started off strong but eventually drifted into her old routine. Amy kept the easel and unfinished canvas up in her living room as a reminder to stick to her promise. After two weeks, the canvas seemed to taunt her. She was scared to put it away and now scared to look at it. She covered the work station with a bed sheet. Eventually, she felt so terrible that she insisted on taking a long-overdue vacation.

Amy binged for five days. Painting non-stop. Oils, watercolors, experimental sloshes, detailed realism, and then a brilliant idea for a painting seemed to come out of nowhere. She worked on the idea with an enthusiasm she hadn't felt in years... Then work called. One of the managers had quit; they needed her to come in.

Weeks went by and she couldn't get back to the painting in a way she felt the work deserved. It began to look uglier and uglier. She couldn't put it away until it seemed to start criticizing her, "You're not an artist. You're a restaurant manager."

Values are not only beliefs that guide our motivation, decisions, and behavior; they also serve as standards of evaluation. When we behave in a manner that is contrary to our values, the healthiest emotion we experience is guilt.

Guilt is intended to be a teaching emotion. It reminds us when our behavior is drifting away from our values. Guilt is an emotion that best serves us when we compassionately listen to it, learn from it, and then let it go. However, we don't naturally manage guilt well. We tend to use this emotion as a shaming stick to beat ourselves up. When that happens, we are vulnerable to our guilt quickly turning into shame, which is guilt personified, moving from "I did badly" to "I am bad." Shame can overwhelm us, which can lead to escapism to avoid the shame, or overcompensation to make up for our behavior. (In this section, we are referring to true guilt, not spurious guilt. Spurious guilt is unfounded guilt related to trauma and abuse. If I grow up in an environment where every day someone tells me, "I'm nothing," I'm eventually going to internalize that. Spurious guilt requires more unpacking in order to differentiate unfounded guilt stemming from trauma and true guilt that arises when our behavior drifts from our values.)

Lee grumbled, "Why can't people just do their jobs? I don't ask anything of anyone that I wouldn't expect of myself." Lee had always been the responsible one. When he was a kid, he held his family together through the divorce. When he was in high school, he was student body president and captain of the baseball team. In college, he dropped out to take care of his mother when she got ill.

He was hired by a plumbing supplies distribution company and eventually worked his way up to a leadership position. Lee's supervisors loved him but he struggled to manage his staff and co-workers. They bristled against his intensity and expectations. Yes, he had high standards for them but he felt they should have already developed those same standards for themselves.

Lee's partner of two years recently broke up with him, saying that he was overly responsible and too judgmental. Lee argued, "Since when did being a responsible person become a bad thing?"

In the same manner that our standards of evaluation can cause us to be oversensitive to our own behavior, we can often turn that evaluation outward, which can cause us to be judgmental of others.

Because values serve as standards of evaluation, it is normal and human for us to see others through the lens of our own values. That lens is never neutral. It is natural for us to feel a negative emotion when we see behavior that conflicts with our values, and it is natural for us to feel a positive emotion when we see behavior that is aligned with our values. If I value Humility and

I see someone showing off or boasting, my first reaction will probably be negative. If you value Objective Analysis and see someone constantly emoting and making emotional decisions, your first reaction will probably be negative. If a group values Concern for Others and sees insensitive, inconsiderate behavior, their first reaction will probably be negative.

When we are in a healthy place, we can understand that initial reactions are normal without drawing conclusions. We can honor our initial reaction but then make an effort not to conclude by remaining actively curious: "What else is true about this person or situation?" Even if we can't answer that question, committing to not making conclusions or judgments gives us a better chance of flourishing in our endeavors. We can have a negative reaction without judging that person. However, when we lead with fear, that process of openness and curiosity shuts down and we punctuate our initial reaction with judgment. Oftentimes we are seeking comfort and it's a lot more comfortable to walk back into the corner of our rightness when somebody is acting differently from what we think is right. We can sit comfortably in the nobility of our rightness and judge. It's a whole lot harder to remain actively curious, learn, and not conclude.

Competing values

Alan was getting increasingly uncomfortable at the weekend parties.

A year ago, he'd finally found a good group of supportive friends. He'd never thought of himself as a "Frat" kind of guy, but this fraternity was different. He was relieved to join a fraternity where the normal stereotypes weren't true. These guys supported each other, challenged each other, and volunteered in the community. They truly knew what it meant to be a brother.

But recently, Alan saw things that bothered him. A couple of the older brothers were going too far at parties. He saw brothers pushing women to aggressively drink beyond the boundaries of sexual consent. Alan wanted to say something but was scared of being ostracized. He hadn't had a reliable group of friends before college, and had now put all of his social capital into his fraternity. If he alienated these guys, what would he do?

The other day, a girl from a recent party came up to his group at lunch and started yelling about something that had happened to her friend. When she left, a couple of brothers made nervous jokes. Alan wanted to say that what was going on wasn't right, but he just sat there…

One of the more stressful situations we can encounter is deciding between two competing values. Take the values Responsibility and Belonging, as in Alan's example. Both are important values to Alan which leaves him susceptible to indecision and inaction. Alan's value of Responsibility deems acting on his value of Belonging as irresponsible, and the importance of Belonging pulls Alan away from acting responsibly for the sake of group acceptance. Contextually, the dilemma of Alan's situation causes Responsibility and

Belonging to compete. Under normal circumstances those same two values might not usually conflict. Strong emotions, such as fear, can cause values to feel equal, when the reality is that values can always be prioritized, moving from what matters to what matters most. Alan clearly knows that what he is observing is disturbing and wrong, but the fear of what will happen to important relationships causes him to hesitate. It has created a "Yes, but..." dilemma for him. His fear compels him to see the two values as equal, when analytically he knows they are not. How do we cultivate the courage to prioritize our values when our emotions make it hard to do so? That is the purpose of programs like Authentic Excellence and Giving Voice to Values.

It is important to understand how and why two values can compete, including values that are inherent competitors such as Independence and Belonging, Achievement and Humility, Responsibility to Self and Concern for Others. If both competing values are important to you, it is difficult to prioritize or choose between two "rights". As with the other vulnerabilities, the issue is not the vulnerability itself but how we tend to naturally manage it. Let's go back to Amy's story. A common vulnerability that she encounters is competition between Financial Responsibility and Creativity.

While Amy was struggling with her guilt over not painting and working long hours at the restaurant, an old acquaintance put her in contact with an individual looking for a portraitist. Amy was asked to paint a portrait of two people for very little money, but the potential networking contacts could lead to more lucrative painting work.

Amy agreed to the job on the spot. "I'll find the time somewhere," she promised herself. However, there was not enough time. No matter how much she reduced sleep, relationships, or restaurant work, she was still late for appointments, hazy at the easel, and technically dull. At the restaurants, the bosses were hesitant to involve her in new ventures. Her friends and partner were concerned.

We naturally tend to manage competing values through over-commitment or indecisiveness. In the moment, it is more comfortable to say "yes" to any opportunity that can satisfy a personal value, because to say "no" to something meaningful feels wrong and is stressful. But by avoiding the stress of saying "no" we become vulnerable to the stress of over-commitment. We can fool ourselves in the fallacy that we'll just make it work, but that ignores the reality of our limited time and energy. By trying to reduce current stress, we often ignore the future burden we place on ourselves.

The Fear-Based Model of Excellence can amplify our vulnerability to indecision and over-commitment. If we become dependent on outcomes to be reassured that we're going to be okay, we create a need to know that the decisions we're making are going to lead to the right outcomes. But we're not omniscient, which can leave us vulnerable to turning imagined outcomes into expected results. If we need outcomes, then decision-making is going to be very stressful and fearful, especially when that opportunity or circumstance involves two competing values to inform our action. We will typically resort to three options: indecisively avoid the decision until we absolutely have to act or the situation evaporates, perpetually over-analyze data until we convince ourselves of the "right" answer, or try to play both sides and over-commit.

It takes courage to prioritize and act despite meaningful conflicts.

When an opportunity or scenario presents itself, we are more likely to flourish when we ask ourselves, "What are the meaningful purposes and benefits associated with this opportunity or scenario?" and "What are the costs?" Before saying yes to any opportunity, even if we know accepting the opportunity will satisfy values, allowing 24 hours to really consider those two questions can lead to more effective decision-making. Chapter 17 explores this further regarding values and decision-making.

In Part II, we will go through the Authentic Excellence training program designed to move beyond the natural challenges associated with the Fear-Based Model of Excellence.

Key points

1. The combination of values-centered living and the fear associated with uncertainty leaves us susceptible to certain vulnerabilities that we naturally don't manage well.
2. Those vulnerabilities are fear of failure, the need for equity and fairness, evaluation in the form of guilt and judgment, and competing values.

Personalizing the concepts

1. When have you found yourself upset over a lack of equity or something unfair happening to you? What was the context and what important value was the unfairness brushing against?
2. When are you vulnerable to being excessively hard on yourself? What is the context and possible value that is triggering that guilt?
3. When do you find yourself vulnerable to being hard on others? What is the context and possible value that is triggering that judgment?
4. What competing values do you find yourself struggling to accommodate most frequently? How do you typically manage that conflict? When does that work well for you and when does it get in your way?

Notes

Part II

Understanding and training for Authentic Excellence

5   Moving beyond our neurology to Authentic Excellence

It had been quite a stressful year of "have to"s leading up to Lena's first year of college. She had always been the rock of the family since her Dad passed away, but the months before college proved to be overwhelming: She was managing the hurdles of financial aid and scholarships, her mother was struggling with separation anxiety and lashing out, she worked full time at a clothing retailer, and she was trying to teach her younger siblings the daily responsibilities they would need to take care of once she was gone.

Lena allowed herself a gift before school started. She had registered for a week-long backpacking trip on the Appalachian Trail. The trip was arranged by Campus Recreation where at the end of each day of hiking Trip Leaders would engage students in conversations about their values, hopes, and fears. Lena typically avoided such conversations because she felt that they were too abstract and ineffective. However, she needed a week before college started to decompress from the stress of home and soak up nature with a small group of other students.

The group spent each day walking many miles spanning several mountains. Amidst the fatigue and sense of accomplishment, the evenings provided a genuine environment for conversation. With each discussion, the trip leaders would emphasize the question, "Why?" They would encourage students to go deeper with "why" in order to get to the purpose of what they found meaningful in the day.

The practice of "why" became the theme of the week, which Lena found to be a welcome relief after years of intense "have to"s. During the last night of the trip, all the various groups who had hiked other sections of the trail met at a large campground for a culminating bonfire. The stories and realizations that were shared solidified the importance of leading with purpose and values, the "why" behind the "what" and "how".

Aside from making friends, feeling less alone in her anxieties, and connecting with nature, the trip surprised Lena by how often she found herself asking, "Why?" At college, the "why" mindset helped her manage the frustration of "having to" make frequent two-hour trips home to help with her family's needs. It was easy to get overwhelmed by the joint to-do list of family and college. However, when she practiced asking, "Why?" she could connect to, "I love my family and I want to help them succeed." This helped her draw from a source of resilience rather than resentment.

During Lena's second semester, she was still going home frequently, and it was getting increasingly difficult to keep resentment and frustration in check. She asked herself, "Why?" Her siblings were stepping up to responsibilities and tasks. Her mother had said that she didn't need Lena to come home as much. "Why was going home still a 'have to'?" The "why" led to some tough truths. Lena suspected that she had wrapped up a lot of her self-worth in being able to take care of her family. Furthermore, taking care of her family provided a valid excuse to avoid new experiences at college that she found intimidating. Asking "why" had outlined a path that would take courage to follow, but "why" would also tether Lena to the underlying purposes and values of why she was following that path. Values like Achievement, Belonging, Creativity, and Privacy could be expressed if she engaged in more opportunities available to her at college.

Part I explored the reasons why it is hard for us to flourish. Our natural reaction to relentless pace, uncertainty, and competition can foster a pattern of thinking that limits us. We can find ourselves living at our neurology (crisis and regulation), where we are primarily motivated by fear and comfort. This can lead to habitual coping patterns of over-control, avoidance, and soothing that serve to calm us but interfere with excellence. How do we move beyond living by the "have to"s of the day, judging ourselves by the outcomes we experience, and seeking comfort in between?

The specific goals of Authentic Excellence aim to deepen a person's level of authenticity, integrity, resilience, and excellence. We have identified five prominent patterns of thinking that facilitate these goals. We refer to these mindsets as paradigm shifts, a different way of thinking that has substantive behavioral and psychological effects. When we flourish, we are not over-thinking; we are deliberate in how we approach the moment. We use the term paradigm shift because most people don't naturally think in a manner that leads to consistent excellence. We have to intentionally put ourselves in the right frame of mind.

Part II, the training program of the Authentic Excellence Initiative, focuses on the following Five Paradigm Shifts to facilitate a deeper level of authenticity, personal integrity, resilience, and excellence.

Shifting from...

1. **Values clarification to values relationship.** In order for values to serve as a consistent source of motivation and behavioral influence, we must go beyond what our values are to a level of interaction with our values that is relational. That interaction involves understanding how our values are alive in our daily functioning, how they manifest in our decision-making and actions, how they interact with each other, and how they cause us fulfillment and stress. In Chapter 6, we explore how to develop a healthy relationship with your values to promote greater effectiveness.
2. **Equity-minded to integrity-minded.** We can define our worth by whether we are getting a fair return on our investment of time and energy. However,

one of the cornerstones of confidence and a healthy self-esteem is a personal sense of integrity—how well our behavior is aligned with our values. To flourish, we must shift from defining our success and worth as a collection of outcomes in the form of equity to defining success and worth by the degree our daily behavior reflects our values. Chapter 7 will help clarify what your values look like in action and distinguish a personal boundary between healthy and unhealthy expressions of those values.

3. **Reducing fear through over-control and avoidance of holding fear well.** Fear-based excellence compels us to manage fear through over-control or avoidance. People who consistently flourish are not less afraid, they hold fear well. They understand that because of uncertainty, fear will always accompany what is important to them. Their objective is to keep fear in perspective so that their values primarily lead their behavior rather than fear. In Chapter 8, we discuss six strategies for managing fear optimally.

4. **Avoidance of difficult emotions to confidence in managing difficult emotions.** We can be highly productive, fulfilled, and resilient, yet still experience difficult emotions like hurt, anger, worry, and guilt. Through no fault of our own, we may encounter loss or failure. How do we thrive through disappointment or heartbreak? When we flourish, we are less concerned about avoiding difficult emotions like hurt and more focused on managing hurt in a healthy manner. Chapter 9 discusses coping and self-care strategies to develop one's confidence in managing difficult emotions.

5. **A chronically evaluative mindset to an expressive mindset.** To flourish, we must shift from constant self-evaluation to a mindset where we are defining our success by the expression of our values. Interestingly, an expressive mindset is the same mindset that promotes the flow or zone state of optimal performance. In Chapter 10, we outline five daily action steps to develop an expressive mindset.

Dynamic Blueprinting

While we have distilled the components of Authentic Excellence to Five Paradigm Shifts, it can still be overwhelming to keep all of the concepts in mind. As you work through the Five Paradigm Shifts, we will provide exercises that personalize these concepts as a blueprint of the most essential components for your mental training. The term "dynamic" represents adjustments and refinements that arise as your environment changes, time passes, and you become more adept at applying and personalizing the concepts.

Training for Authentic Excellence

Step 1

The First Paradigm Shift deals with the importance of moving from values clarification to a relationship with your values. This involves first clarifying what values are important to you and how they then manifest and interact in the context of your daily life.

Our non-profit organization, Life Values Inventory Online, provides an online values assessment tool that is an open educational resource free and unrestricted to the general public. We have also provided a hard copy of the assessment in Appendix A at the back of the book. We encourage you to utilize the website, www.lifevaluesinventory.org, as it is more user-friendly, interactive, and takes less time to complete. It also securely stores your results so you can compare your values over time. It is important for you to go through the assessment because your LVI results are the cornerstone for Authentic Excellence training.

Please complete the following steps before proceeding to Chapter 6.

1. Go to www.lifevaluesinventory.org or Appendix A.
2. If you use the website, you can review the introductory pages that describe the philosophy and research associated with the program and the steps taken to ensure your privacy.
3. When ready to go through the assessment, create your account.
4. The LVI assessment consists of five steps. Complete Steps 1–3, reading the instructions carefully because we ask you to think of values a bit differently. It takes 15–20 minutes to complete Steps 1–3.
5. Step 4 generates your Values Profile. Download your results as a PDF file to print or view on your computer or other device. Have your Values Profile available as you proceed through the subsequent chapters.

Key points

1. We have a natural tendency to live at our neurology (crisis and regulation) by focusing our daily actions on "have to"s and comfort.
2. We have defined Five Paradigm Shifts that can help us move beyond our neurology to a deeper level of authenticity, integrity, resilience, and excellence.
3. Dynamic Blueprinting is a process to help personalize and internalize the Five Paradigm Shifts.

Personalizing the concepts

1. Over the past six months, how would you describe your level of productivity, fulfillment, and resilience in each of your important life roles (e.g., work, relationships, leisure)?
2. What factors, both internal and external, led to flourishing and what factors got in the way for each of your important life roles?
3. After completing the LVI assessment and reading your profile, what three things stood out to you the most and why?

Notes

6 Paradigm Shift 1

Shifting from values clarification to values relationship

The staff meeting was stale and the boss's questions were predictable.

"Carol, what value would you say best describes you?"

"Responsibility."

Stefan leaned over to his work buddy and whispered, "That's why she is never happy with anything we do."

"Stefan," the boss interrupted, "what value best describes you?"

"Belonging."

Carol, Stefan's manager, thought to herself, "That's why he spends all his time talking to other people instead of doing his work."

"Ok good. Those are two values that are definitely represented at TeleCorp. We strive to be responsible in our pursuit to help people feel like they belong to a community. One that TeleCorp…" The staff glazed over as the boss continued.

Two weeks later, a good amount of people from the office showed up for Sharon's birthday party. Karaoke had begun. Stefan and Carol found themselves on the outskirts unwilling to participate.

"Not big on Karaoke, huh?" Stefan attempted to socialize with Carol.

"There aren't enough drinks in the world to get me up there."

"Same here. I'm gonna get a drink. Do you want one?"

"Sure, I got a sitter for the night."

"I didn't know you had kids."

"A daughter. She's six."

"That's amazing. You have a picture?"

Carol reluctantly pulled out her phone and showed Stefan a picture of her daughter. Stefan was overwhelmed when he saw the picture of Carol's daughter in a wheelchair. He thought about all the times he had made fun of Carol for being too uptight and responsible.

"She has Cerebral Palsy." Stefan froze in shame. Carol rescued, "It's ok not to say anything. She's great."

"No, I'm sure she is… I was just… I mean…"

"It's ok… Relax."

"I'm sorry."

"Don't be."

"…I don't do well when I don't know what to say."

"Why do you feel you have to say something?"

"I don't feel pressure to say some-thing. I feel pressure to say the right thing."

"Why?"

"I want people to like me." Carol thought about all the times she had gotten frustrated with Stefan for helping other people instead of doing his own work. Stefan continued, *"I spend too much time trying to get people to like me. I'm helping Carter move this weekend; Sharon's birthday tonight; I promised Nick I'd hang out with him tomorrow… It's too much."*

"You can say 'no'."

"I'm just not used to it."

"Don't try so hard."

"I'm working on it. I'm learning to let go…"

"Old habits die hard."

Later that night Carol thought about how she'd always forced herself to be responsible so that people would take her seriously. Maybe it was time to let some of that go.

Later that night Stefan thought about how hard Carol worked to take care of her daughter. He felt inspired to work harder at his job for the greater purpose of maybe one day owning his own business.

To be consistently and optimally effective, we must move beyond our natural sources of motivation—fear and comfort. Our values are attached to authentic purpose so they provide a deeper form of motivation, but only if those values are active in our lives. Just knowing our values is not enough. In fact, *values clarification alone can often lead to frustration because we know enough to judge ourselves and others, but have not engaged our values deeply enough to tap into that motivation.*

In order for values to serve as a consistent source of motivation and behavioral influence, we must develop a deeper, relational understanding of our values. What does it mean to have a relationship with your values? Like all relationships, it means to routinely prioritize the importance values have in your life, to be aware of their influence instead of taking them for granted, to be actively engaged by acting on them, and to take time to appreciate the meaning they have in your life. For example, how would your behavior show an observer that you have a healthy relationship with your partner? Similarly, how would an observer know that a value is important to you based on your behavior?

Think of your healthiest relationships. You have the clarification of who those people are in your life (e.g., your friend, partner, sibling, parent), but that says little about the quality of the relationship. With our healthiest relationships, we are actively engaged with the other party and periodically check in to see how the relationship is developing. The same process is necessary to move beyond a clarification of your values to a place where they are healthy and consistently motivational.

Having a relationship with your values also means understanding the nuances and complexities of how they are a part of your life. For instance, how are your values interacting with each other? What's fulfilling and stressful about your values? How are your values expressed in life roles (e.g., work, leisure, relationships)? How are your values influencing how you interact with the world around you?

Before we move into questions that help build a relationship with our values, let's review what you have clarified. Using the LVI assessment tool (located at www.lifevalueinventory.org or Appendix A), you have already developed a profile of your current relationship with your values. This is a step beyond values clarification, but more reflection can further strengthen the relationship.

Exercise: Getting to know your values

Coupled with your LVI Values Profile, spend some time reflecting on the following questions.

Reflections on your high priority values

- What's great and positive about having these values high in your ranking?
- What's stressful about having these values high in your ranking?
- What were the influences that shaped these values (e.g., cultural or generational influences)?
- How do these values get expressed? How would others know that they are important to you? What does a healthy expression of these values look like for you?
- How new or old do these values feel for you? Would they have been among your top values a few years ago? Do you think they will be your top values a few years from now?
- How do your High Priority values compare to others in your family, your friends, and your current community?
- What fears are attached to your most important values and how do you manage/cope with those fears?
- What values feel most comfortable to express in your current environment? What values do your current environment positively affirm?
- What values feel most difficult to express in your current environment? What values do your current environment marginalize or devalue?

Reflections on all 14 values

- What value is currently causing you the most fulfillment and why?
- What value is currently causing you the most stress and why?
- What value has changed the most for you in the last year?
- What value do you hope to affect the most in the next year and how?
- What value do you gravitate to during times of change or extreme stress? How does that work well for you, and how does it present challenges?

- What personal value(s) reflect your family culture and what value(s) represent a departure?
- By what value(s) are you hardest on yourself and others in terms of judgment?
- If you could only be remembered for two values, what would they be and how are they currently expressed?
- Look at your Over-Attended values. Why are you acting on these values more than you would prefer? What are the underlying purposes calling you to act on these values?
- If you could only choose one, what value in your Under-Attended category would you be willing to devote a little more time and energy to?
- Are there values in your Medium/Low Priority category that you feel are negatively judged by others because of their lower importance? Where is that judgment coming from and why?
- Are there relationships where a Low Priority value for you is a High Priority value for others? How do you navigate that difference in values priority in the relationship?

Further considerations

Imagine you take a friend you care about to dinner. You both spend hours talking about what's important in your life right now, the challenges and stresses you regularly face, and the strengths and triumphs you're proud of. You also look at ways to help each other and interact together. This meeting will have an impact because you can't unlearn the meaningful aspects you discovered about the other person. If you committed to meeting 1–2 times a year, it would deepen the meaning of that relationship and influence your actions and motivation. We learned that this type of meeting with one's values is a common practice among people who flourish. They commit to reflecting 1–2 times a year on what matters most to them and how those values are demonstrated in their behavior. They use that reflection to create a foundation for the year's motivation and decision-making.

Why does this matter? If we were to observe your behavior for a month, we would quickly learn what is important to you and how you manage fear. If throughout the day we were to ask you every few minutes, "Why are you doing that?" there would be times when you would respond, "Because if I don't, I'm afraid x will happen." There would be other times when you would respond, "Because I believe it's right for me to do." With every decision you make, you have a choice to lead with fear or lead with your values. When you lead with fear, you're more likely to plateau. When you lead with values, you're more likely to flourish. By developing a deeper relationship with your values, you are more likely to pull your values to the foreground when making decisions, which increases the probability of living with purpose instead of living at your neurology, our patterned responses to managing pressure by leading with fear and comfort.

Story connection

Stories help us internalize and understand experiences with greater depth. The questions in this chapter are intended to help you create a story. Deep, healthy relationships have stories attached to them. Ask a person to describe a relationship and then ask that person to tell a story about the relationship; there will often be a difference in the way the person will engage or express a sense of meaning. We want the same level of engagement and meaning with your values.

As we go through life, it is important to reassess each year how our experiences integrate to inform us about who we are and where we want to go. These stories shape our relationship with our values and influence our decision-making. But, in the same manner that a good story begs to be shared with others, it's important to share the reflections of your values with someone else and inquire about their values-relationship stories. When you organize your thoughts into a conversational story that others understand, you move into another level of understanding. And when you ask the same questions of others, hear their stories, and reflect on the impact of those stories, you move into an even deeper level of understanding with your own values. This deepening of comprehension through story increases the probability that your values will become your primary source of motivation. A motivation that surpasses mood, fatigue, and fear. Understanding the story of your values relationship calls for your values to lead and your fear to follow, in a world where the reverse is common.

Values categories

In tandem with your LVI Values Profile, let's take a closer look at the four different values categories. In understanding these categories, we can learn important elements about our values, which can strengthen our relationship with them.

High Priority values

High Priority values are the values that are currently important to you and that you act on frequently. These are values of integrity because you're walking the walk and acting on what matters to you. They are a source of fulfillment and meaning at this time in your life. However, values are a double-edged sword because they are our highest source of fulfillment, but they are also a high source of stress. It's important to have well-established stress management skills (which we cover in later chapters) in order for these values to foster flourishing and meaning.

We are also vulnerable to needing equity from our High Priority values. These values are important to us and we are putting in the effort to frequently act on them. It's natural to want a return on that investment of time, energy, and care. The key is to want a fair return without needing it or feeling entitled to it. Otherwise, fear starts to slide to the foreground and your values start to move into a need state.

Over-Attention values

Over-Attention values are values that you are currently devoting more attention to than you would prefer. We often experience more stress from these values than joy. For very real and understandable reasons, fear is leading with these values and there can be a level of insecurity or worry attached to them. The fear is not irrational and the insecurity is come by honestly. Through past or current life experiences, you may have more doubt in your relationship with these values than trust. It may be an insecurity that you have carried for years or it may be a current life situation that is causing you to feel less secure about a particular value.

Oftentimes we devote more attention to a value than we'd prefer for a greater right. We are choosing to be in a situation that carries a burden or consequence that results in over-attention to a particular value. Like Carol's example at the beginning of the chapter, a parent may over-attend to the value of Responsibility because their child is managing a serious illness, but it is an acceptable burden for the greater rightness of caring for their child.

We are vulnerable to feeling insecure about a value when we are outcome-oriented and don't feel confident in our ability to secure that outcome. We can excessively worry about the outcome, which is a form of over-attention. Whenever we're devoting more attention to a value than we would prefer, the outcome can start to feel like a "have to" or a need, which elevates stress.

With Over-Attention values, it's important to objectively understand the "why" behind devoting more attention to a value than you would prefer. When we objectively look at the "why" we can get to the underlying purpose or "rightness" that calls us to take on the burden of over-attention. For example, "I'm spending more time on Responsibility than I prefer because it is more important for me to help my family right now." Or, "I want to run my own business one day so I'm having to focus more on Financial Prosperity than I'd prefer." Or, in reference to Alan's example in Chapter 4, "I want to stand up against sexual assault which requires me to focus on expressing my value of Responsibility not Belonging right now." The "why" can help us be resilient and respect the reasons that drive our over-attention. Objectively asking "why" can also help us expose and readjust insecurities that drive Over-Attention values. "Why do I always feel like I "have to" be helping my friends? Maybe my value of Belonging is in the Over-Attention category because I'm insecure that people won't like me if I don't constantly help them." Or, "Why do I need to do well in this audition? Because if I don't get this part, people will think I'm a bad actor. Am I over-attending to my value of Creativity because my identity is too attached to it?"

If you could magically detach fear and insecurity from an Over-Attention value, would it move to a High Priority value (one that is still important and that you would act on frequently) or a Medium/Low Priority value (moderate importance that you would act on periodically)? The question is designed to help you gain a sense of how central this value needs to remain in your life. Is this a time in your life when you may be able to influence the insecurity or fear that is attached to this value? How can you make changes to do so? If not, remember that you are choosing to have this Over-Attention value active in your life for important reasons. So it is necessary to develop and apply healthy coping strategies for the stress these values can cause until you feel you have more autonomy to influence change.

Under-Attention values

Your Under-Attention values are values that you are devoting less attention to than you would prefer. We tend to experience guilt or sadness around these values. There are typically two reasons why we put values into this category. First, it can be because we are truthfully devoting less time to a value than we believe we should. Second, we are applying a perfectionistic standard to a value. We are seeing that value in terms of its potential in our lives: "Well, I could always be more humble, or more healthy, or more responsible." The problem is that when we hold ourselves to a perfectionistic standard with our values, we're always falling short. This can lead to harsh self-judgment against that standard on a daily basis. That judgment can turn into chronic guilt, which wears on us to the point of depression or over-compensation. If you have values in the Under-Attention category because you are holding a perfectionistic standard to them, what category would those values fall into if you removed that standard? Base your answer on frequency of behavior. If you frequently act on that value, move it to High Priority. If you periodically act on that value, move it to Medium/Low Priority.

Let's look at the values remaining in the Under-Attention category because you are truly devoting less attention to these values than you would prefer. If you could only pick one value from that list to devote more energy to, what would it be? The time and energy it takes to healthfully manage our High Priority and Over-Attention values leaves very little energy for other values. Furthermore, Under-Attention values require a level of fight and commitment to act on. Something inhibits our ability to naturally act on these values or there isn't a critical need to act on them. Otherwise, these values would be in the High Priority or Over-Attention category. Under-Attention values require a motivational fight to commit more time to them, and we only have so much fight in us after managing other important values. We are more likely to flourish when we commit to fighting for one Under-Attention value and accept that the others will go under-attended for a while. This perspective helps us avoid languishing in the guilt of our failure to act on all of our Under-Attention values. Rather than blame our lack of will-power, we are relating to these values through a healthy assessment of our time and energy.

Medium/Low Priority values

Like the High Priority values, your Medium/Low Priority values are currently in a place of integrity. Your behavior is aligned with their relative import- ance. Relative to other values, these values have moderate to low importance in your life right now, and you are comfortable acting on them periodically. However, sometimes these values can create challenges when you are in an environment where you are judged negatively for seeing a value as medium to low priority, or when you are in a relationship with someone who has a High Priority value that is medium to low priority for you. Both require awareness, healthy coping strategies, and active empathy to manage the gap between the different perspectives.

Key points

1. In order for values to serve as a consistent influence on our behavior and a strong source of motivation, we must move from values clarification to a deeper, relational understanding of our values.
2. It's important to annually or semi-annually extensively reflect on how your values are currently alive in your life. It's equally important to share those reflections with someone and ask about their values.
3. Categorizing values as High Priority, Over-Attention, Under-Attention, and Medium/Low Priority helps us objectively assess time and energy in relationship to our values, which increases our likelihood of flourishing.

Notes

7 Paradigm Shift 2
Shifting from equity-minded to integrity-minded

He couldn't wait to get his fingers on the strings of the guitar. His left hand glided up and down the frets with the perfect amount of pressure and vibrato. His right hand struck, plucked, tickled, and strummed the strings to sing colors and textures. Leo's ear conducted while his fingers danced over the instrument like a kid on a jungle gym. There were no scales. There were no chords. No patterns or shapes. Just play and sound. Every note worked. Every motif created a new adventure. Leo played his guitar.

Karla could step out of herself and into this new person. A new role. A new character. A new being. She fell in love with this new person. Karla connected to her pain. She connected to her cunning. She imagined backstories and let them solidify as memories. How would the character's wrist move when she was scared? How did that feel? Karla fell inside that feeling. Maybe a slight French accent would be fun. Karla reveled in the playing of another person. Honoring another being. Bringing life to an imagined idea. She could scream with all the character's pain like she never could in her own life. She could cry, laugh, taunt, torture, or love as an actor, acting... becoming someone else.

Leo couldn't wait until the gig was over. He worried that the new band members thought he wasn't a good guitar player. Would the audience be impressed with the solos he had planned out? On the train ride over he reviewed the chord progressions of each song that he thought he'd memorized. What if he forgot during the show? The gig started and he kept trying to remember the right chords, the right scales, the right melodies. Leo forced complex fingerings of chord structures hoping people would notice, but he found himself off beat and hitting sour notes. During his solo, everything seemed to fall flat. The air went out of the balloon and he struggled to stay with the band's momentum. Every note sounded wrong. He tried to remember shapes and scale patterns, but his fingers were terrified of the fretboard.

Karla worried that her performance was boring. Where was all that passion in rehearsal? Screaming the character's pain. Laughing the character's triumph. It felt like she was reading a bank statement. The audience wasn't responding. The well-known director of the play would probably find her performance to be as memorable as a bland breakfast. Did she say that line right? All her deliveries seemed stale. The other actors must be thinking this was her first play.

In the middle of Leo's solo, he decided to focus on having fun with just two notes. He started to feel his fingers on the strings. He fell back into the rhythm. The charts and scales began to melt away. There was sound again and he allowed himself to be taken with it. No wrong notes, just sound and play. The audience saw Leo go from safe and scared to hearing something interesting that pulled them back into the music, Leo's music, their music.

Karla remembered that she loved the character's sharp wit. How many times in Karla's life had she failed to think of a timely comeback? Not this character. This new being always had a counterpunch. Karla let go of herself and relished the battery of perfumed insults her character was scripted to unleash on the others. There was no delivery to mess up. No lines to perform. Just becoming a character that she loved. The audience had struggled to follow the scene until they were suddenly swept up in this awakened character. The play came to life.

Now that you have developed a deeper understanding of your current values, how do you act on these values on a daily basis?

It's too exhausting to process the depths of your values relationships every day. Conversely, important insights can evaporate if there is no effort made to internalize them. We can benefit from a middle ground between over-analysis and inattention to allow our deeper understanding to then inform how we act within the context of the day.

This chapter is designed to clarify what your values look like in action and to establish a personal boundary between healthy and unhealthy expressions of those values. Why does this require a paradigm shift? We most naturally think of our values by how we experience them. If I value Belonging, how well am I experiencing a sense of connection to others? If I value Achievement, how well am I accomplishing what I want? The Fear-Based Model of Excellence compels us to define our worth by whether we are getting a fair return on our investment of time, energy, and care. These factors create a strong pull on how we perceive and manage our values. It moves us to start defining our self-esteem by the return we are getting on our efforts and by the evaluations of others. Unfortunately, these factors contradict an important component of self-esteem and resilience.

One of the cornerstones of adult self-esteem is a personal sense of integrity, of how well our behavior is aligned with our values. They are never perfectly aligned but when our behavior reflects what is important to us, we feel good about ourselves and manage stress in a resilient manner. When our behavior drifts from our values, we suffer. Sometimes the suffering is acceptable, but the more our behavior drifts from what matters to us, the more we will need to manage that discomfort through soothing that may or may not be healthy. To flourish, we must shift from defining our success and worth as a collection of equitable outcomes to defining success and worth by the degree our daily behavior reflects our values. Crystallizing what our values look like in action, and clarifying the boundaries between unhealthy and healthy expression fosters this level of integrity. *Equity matters; expression has to matter more.*

Once we turn down the noise of equity and give more worth to personal integrity, we also become more attuned to any internal conflicts that may be getting in the way. Being integrity-minded moves us to a deeper level of awareness. Take Amy's situation in Chapter 4. She was finally able to courageously devote time and value to her painting regardless of whether others saw it or not. But her internal guilt kept her from truly enjoying and deriving worth from the expression, preventing her from seeing that her behavior was healthy. The point is, we can't even get to this deeper level of tuning into our internal conflicts until we shift from being equity-minded to integrity-minded. It's similar to someone who abuses alcohol and stops drinking. Stopping the destructive coping pattern of abusing alcohol is healthy. But now they have to face the underlying reasons that were driving them to drink in the first place. It's necessary work but work that could not have happened until the drinking stopped. Addressing underlying issues then provides the opportunity for healthy behavior to be more consistent in one's life. Being integrity-minded doesn't resolve all of the obstacles of flourishing, but it's a necessary step to be able to understand and address personal inhibitors. Once that happens, the likelihood of consistent values-congruent behavior is enhanced.

Dynamic Blueprint exercise: Your values in action

To shift from thinking of your values in terms of equity, it can be helpful to develop concrete examples of what your values look like in action and when they are expressed in a healthy or unhealthy manner. The reason is pretty simple. The pressures of life do not foster flourishing; they drift us from it. For the reasons explained in Part I, the world often pulls us to express our values in unhealthy ways. But if we have a clear understanding of what unhealthy expressions of our values look like, we can recognize when the world pulls us in that direction. Similarly, if we define what healthy expressions of our values look like, we have a better idea of where to go when we drift into unhealthy forms of expression. If I quickly become aware that I am drifting into unhealthy expression and have an idea of what healthy expression looks like, I can immediately choose healthy. When we flourish, our motivation to manage the noise of the world is less about prevention and more about accepting an ongoing level of catching and recovering.

Your values in action

Returning to your LVI Values Profile, take a look at each value starting with your High Priority values. Write out what your values look like in action when they are healthy and when they are unhealthy. This exercise is about defining how your values manifest in daily life. Therefore, it helps to focus on your behavior rather than the outcomes of your actions. Secondly, write out the life role or roles where you typically express each value. Some examples of life roles are work, education, family, and leisure. What "hat(s)" are you wearing when you're acting on a value?

Examples

Value: Concern for others

> *Healthy expression: Balancing between sensitivity to others and self-care; understanding first, helping second.*
> *Unhealthy expression: Feeling responsible for others' wellbeing; putting others' needs first; rushing to help.*
> *Life role(s) when acting on this value: Work, friendships, relationships, community service.*

Value: Creativity

> *Healthy expression: Focusing on the imagination and play of creating. Connecting to the senses involved in the medium and the expression. Participating in a creative work 4–5 times a week.*
> *Unhealthy expression: Chronically assessing the impression my perform-ance or work has on an audience or peers. Defining my self-worth by the perceived quality of my creative work. Too preoccupied with delivering my creative expressions the "correct" way.*
> *Life role(s) when acting on this value: Work, leisure.*

Value: Health and activity

> *Healthy expression: Doing something each day for my health and wellbeing, whether it's exercise, meditation, or mindful eating.*
> *Unhealthy expression: Exercising to excess in order to feel in control or to attain a perfectionistic body type as defined by society. Avoiding exer-cise for several weeks and consuming to excess because I am putting too much pressure on myself.*
> *Life role(s) when acting on this value: Leisure.*

Category effect

Defining, or blueprinting, what healthy expressions of our High Priority values look like clarifies the deeper meaning of these values. We are reminded why these values are important to us, which increases motivation through pur-pose rather than results or equity.

Blueprinting our Over-Attention values is important even when we are unable to express those values in a healthy way. Other factors are influencing our Over-Attention values, but having a picture of what healthy expression looks like for us increases the probability of being able to step into that healthy expression when possible.

We benefit from blueprinting our Under-Attention and Medium/Low Priority values because it shows us how periodically acting on certain values is a healthy assessment of our time and energy. For some of these values, a healthy expression may be a few minutes each week, once a month, or even annually. These values are still alive in our life, but we are acting on them in a manner that respects the priorities in our life and the limitations of our time and energy.

Macro perspective

You've blueprinted what healthy and unhealthy expressions of each value look like in action. Now let's look at things through a wider lens. Where would you mark your current overall expression of each value on a continuum of healthy/unhealthy expression? Remember to focus on your behavior, not the outcomes of your actions.

Examples

Value: Concern for Others

    Healthy expression ------------X-----------|-------------- Unhealthy expression

Value: Creativity

    Healthy expression ----------------|---X----------------- Unhealthy expression

Value: Health and Activity

    Healthy expression ------X----------------|-------------- Unhealthy expression

Now from a macro perspective, consider the values together instead of separately. Make any refinements or adjustments based on that wider lens. For example, when considering your Health and Activity value alone, you may have written that you want to exercise five times a week for an hour. But as you consider the other values and their time commitments, it may be healthier to modify that expression to three times a week for 30 minutes. As you look at your blueprint through a broader lens, are there any noticeable trends on the continuums of healthy/unhealthy expression? Are you pretty healthy overall with your values expressions or is there a trend toward unhealthy expression?

This blueprint is not a to-do list. It is intended to be a reference to start thinking differently about your values. It's a reminder that flourishing is tied to expression, and knowing what your values look like during daily expression matters. Shifting from the plateau effects of equity to the flourishing effects of integrity involves defining the worth of your day by your expression of values rather than by outcomes. It's okay to be in a better mood when you get equitable outcomes and it's okay to be sad or upset when you don't, but it shouldn't impact your self-worth. Hang your self-worth on the expression of your values. Everything else requires other factors beyond your control. Paradoxically, you increase the likelihood of experiencing more positive outcomes when you focus more on expression.

As you look at your blueprint, do you notice any common components that differentiate healthy expression from unhealthy expression? The elements of healthy expression often center around purpose, process, and realistic estimations of time and energy. Healthy expression is the pursuit of integrity, which is driven by courage. It is hard to define your worth by the alignment of your behavior with your values when there is so much pressure to define your worth by outcomes and the evaluations of others. With unhealthy expression, you will tend to notice that the focus is more on control, emotional comfort, natural habits, outcomes, and comparison to others. It's the pursuit of equity, which is driven by need.

Cognitive strain/cognitive ease

Ray and his wife, April, saw a group of young people boisterously causing trouble in a local grocery store. He vented to April, "Young people today are out of control. This world is doomed."

"I do not like it when you generalize things like that. Many kids of every generation have acted like that, and some are probably acting out of insecurity trying to belong… It's not a simple stereotype."

"Sometimes it is."

"You complain about how your mother is always making assumptions and judgments. You've got to question yourself and accept complexity if you don't want to act like her."

Later, as they waited to check out, April overheard some people speaking Spanish. She asked Ray, "Why don't you take Spanish lessons with me again?"

"You're way ahead of me."

"I don't mind starting over. You were too hard on yourself last time."

"I couldn't remember any conjugations."

"It gets easier. You don't have to try and memorize everything. Just watch a couple of TV shows in Spanish with me."

One of the teens from the rowdy group approached Ray, "'Scuse me, I think you dropped your wallet."

The young person handed Ray the wallet. "…Thank you."

When the teen walked away, Ray instinctually checked to find that his cash and credit cards were still there. He looked at April. "It's time for me to learn something new."

The combined power of the first two paradigm shifts impacts a psychological concept known as cognitive strain/cognitive ease (Kahneman, 2011). Cognitive strain is when we are paying very careful attention to what we are doing. Cognitive ease is when we're paying casual attention to what we're doing. When we encounter or learn something new, we are in a place of cognitive strain. Cognitive strain is a healthy state because it fosters our growth and development, but it's also unsustainable to consistently stay in a place of cognitive strain. We naturally seek cognitive ease. So we develop patterns and habits to incorporate cognitive ease into our daily behavior such as generalizations, predictions, and assumptions. Unchecked, cognitive ease can create challenges for us. It can lead us to develop biased or stereotypical patterns of thinking that cause us to overlook details or differences that challenge those patterns of thinking. It's similar when we seek to move beyond our neurology. Managing our fear of failure through over-control or avoidance is a form of cognitive ease because it is what our neurological system is designed to do when we lead with fear. To move away from that pattern of behavior requires shifting to a place of cognitive strain. The training of the first two paradigm shifts causes cognitive strain initially, but it interrupts the patterns of cognitive ease that keep us controlling and avoiding. By dipping into cognitive strain for a brief period with these exercises, you develop a deeper understanding and connection to your values, which eventually moves them to a place of cognitive ease. When your values move into a place of cognitive ease, it increases the likelihood that you will use your values to guide your behavior instead of fear or comfort. To reduce the vulnerability of values drifting too far into patterned behavior, you only need to commit to doing these exercises on an annual basis and during important transitions.

Key points

1. One of the cornerstones of adult self-esteem is a sense of personal integrity—the alignment of our behavior with our values.
2. Integrity is difficult because we tend to think of our values in terms of how we experience them through outcomes, equity. However, we can benefit by defining integrity in terms of how we express our values through our behavior. The experience and outcomes stemming from our values are important; they matter, but expression has to matter more in order to flourish.
3. The paradigm shift is to derive your worth primarily from the expression of your values rather than the outcomes of the day. The presence or absence of outcomes may impact our mood or emotions, but they shouldn't be so personalized that they affect our self-worth.

4. Shifting from equity to integrity is difficult in this competitive and comparative world, which is why it can help to view this hard work as courageous.
5. The combination of the first two paradigm shifts creates a deeper understanding and connection to our values moving that connection from cognitive strain toward cognitive ease. That cognitive ease in relating to our values increases the probability that our values will become our primary source of motivation, instead of fear or comfort.

Personalizing the concepts

1. Take time to recall and appreciate where you are currently expressing your values in a healthy manner.
2. Take time to better understand (not judge) the factors or triggers that move you toward unhealthy expressions.

Reference

Kahneman, D. (2011). *Thinking, fast and slow*. New York: Farrar, Straus and Giroux.

Notes

8   Paradigm Shift 3

Shifting from fear reduction to holding fear well

There is a dynamic relationship between values and fear. When you dare to care about something, stakes become involved. Many of us are taught how to care, but not how to manage the fear associated with caring. Fear-based excellence brings fear to the foreground to kick-start the nervous system into action through over-control or avoidance. Does that mean when people flourish they are less afraid? No, they hold fear well. People who manage fear well understand that because of uncertainty fear will always accompany what is important to them. The objective is to keep fear in perspective so that values stay in the foreground. In this chapter, we discuss six strategies for managing fear of failure optimally. The goal of each of these strategies is to move fear into its sweet spot, where it keeps us alert but is not our primary driver.

Rethinking fear of failure

***Strategy #1: Moving from perceiving fear as an emotion
of threat to an emotion of importance***

Emma had enjoyed a stellar career in gymnastics, attaining almost every accolade one could receive in the sport. Now at the age of 25, she was considered too old for gymnastics and decided to transition to golf, which was less age restrictive. She trained for a year before qualifying for her first competition. At the event, she was asked by a reporter if she was more nervous about the golf tournament than when she competed in gymnastics. "Yes, that's the point. What I love most about competing is the thrill of stepping into something important without any guarantees."

Fear is an uncomfortable emotion, both physically and mentally. The unpleasant "what if" scenarios we can formulate in our mind make it very easy to see fear as an emotion of threat. One of the distinctions we found when analyzing people who consistently flourish is that they process the emotion of fear differently. They see it as an emotion associated with importance, confirming that they are engaged in meaningful behavior. They get worried if they are not feeling the pressure associated with fear of failure.

When we flourish we accept and embrace fear as a necessary companion to living a values-based life.

Why does this shift in perspective work in our favor? When fear is viewed as an emotion of threat, it looms large. It feels too overwhelming to overcome, which triggers our patterned reaction of over-control and avoidance. We become preoccupied with being less afraid and, therefore, fear becomes the focus of our attention. When fear reduction becomes our primary focus, the courage that it takes to overcome it feels beyond us. However, seeing fear as a positive emotion that is associated with being engaged in meaning and purpose changes our focus of attention. We become more focused on the meaning rather than the fear. We now only see the endeavor as hard, but a worthwhile hard. Once that happens, the perception of courage also changes. The courage associated with doing something hard and meaningful feels much more approachable than the courage associated with doing something unafraid. Learning to embrace the feeling of fear while stepping onto a path that is right for you is more effective than waiting to be unafraid. The most effective way to change behavior is not by trying to reduce something negative but to increase something positive. Giving Voice to Values (Gentile, 2010), for example, endorses habit formation of frequent values-congruent behaviors so that confidence builds to where such action feels less huge, less courageous. The intention of this habit formation is not to eliminate fear but to shift the focus to increasing positive behaviors and the positive emotions that stem from positive behavior. Seeing fear as an emotion associated with personal importance can shift us from the need to distance ourselves from fear and focus instead on meaning.

Strategy #2: Moving from perceiving failure as a personal statement to an experience of worthy disappointment

Bill received his 200 Hour Yoga Teacher's Training Certificate. He had become disillusioned with his career in finance and wanted to explore his deepening interest in yoga. Bill felt yoga had saved his life. He suffered from depression and chronic back pain which yoga had transformed into manageable challenges. Bill wanted to share the healing power he had experienced and decided to make the career change from finance to teaching yoga.

The difficulty of the 200 Hour Training made him question his ability to teach yoga. However, he was able to get a job at a nearby yoga studio.

After eight months of teaching yoga, Bill still struggled to build up a regular following like the other teachers had done. Despite inconsistent attendance, he felt good about the classes he was conducting and enjoyed going to work.

The owner of the yoga studio was under financial pressure. A luxury gym and another yoga studio had opened in town. The owner was struggling to compete. It was clear that she needed to increase her occasional teaching schedule, expand other teachers' schedules, and let go of two teachers. She didn't want to fire Bill, but the other teachers had been at the studio longer and had larger followings.

Bill took the layoff hard. "I'm not good a teacher. This was a terrible mistake. I can't do the poses like teachers should be able to. My sequencing, my music playlists, my social media posts... nothing works. I have no business being a yoga teacher."

The fear of not attaining the outcomes we work so hard for can become very personal. When we experience "failure" it's very easy to attach future implications to that failure experience. "What does this bad grade mean for my future desire to be a physician?" "What does this rejected manuscript mean for my future as a writer?" "What does this breakup mean for my ability to find a partner?" It's normal to place future meaning on present outcomes. But when we personalize failure, it sharply amplifies our fear. To keep fear in its proper perspective, it is important to see unattained outcomes as worthy disappointments. When people flourish they honor the sting of disappointing outcomes, and they don't see it as anything more than that. They try to learn from disappointing outcomes without concluding personal or future implications. To see something as a personal failure is overwhelming and brings the fear of experiencing failure to the foreground. Perceiving failure as a worthy disappointment can help because humans tend to be more confident in their ability to manage and process disappointment. People feel less confident in processing failure and personal conclusions which oftentimes require special coping strategies.

Strategy #3: Moving from perceiving hurt as awful (requiring protection) to viewing hurt only as difficult

Neal was torn. He had grown to really like Adam and wanted to tell him how he felt. But Neal didn't have the best track record with dating. He tended to fall hard and fast, and would get hurt when the feelings weren't reciprocated. Last year's breakup was especially difficult, and the pain still lingered. To go through another experience like that would be awful. Neal thought Adam had similar feelings, but Adam was shy and difficult to read. What if Neal was wrong about Adam's feelings? Maybe it would be safer to remain friends and keep his feelings to himself.

No one likes to feel hurt, but when we see hurt as an awful thing, we become preoccupied with avoiding it at all costs. This sends fear to the foreground. To flourish, we must deconstruct hurt and see it for what it truly is, a difficult emotion. If we accept hurt as hard, and nothing more than hard, we become less afraid of it. We never like hurt, but if we categorize it as hard and not awful, then it doesn't get in our way as much. Values can lead when the only risk is processing something difficult.

Many people, especially those in marginalized communities, experience reoccurring hurt stemming from systemic prejudice. This strategy is not meant to diminish the validity of that hurt nor to undermine the difficulty of processing that hurt. The point of this strategy is to break up the pain of chronic hurt into temporary periods of varying intensity. In doing so, the goal is to help prevent one's life from being obstructed by chronic protection from hurt.

Strategy #4: Shifting from experiential confidence to volitional confidence

"Jay, can you get to the studio in an hour?"

"An hour?! Will I have any time to rehearse?"

"Probably not, but the backup trumpet player's backup is stuck in traffic."

"Ok, I'll be there."

The gig of a lifetime and Jay had no time to prepare. Since his friend had become an associate producer at a popular late-night show, Jay had hoped he'd get a call to play in the band… but not like this.

Jay was a cerebral player. He was gifted with incredible range, intonation, and comprehension of advanced theory. However, he wasn't a confident impro-viser and struggled to trust his ear. Jay felt more confident when he prepared and rehearsed. Now the biggest gig of his life had come and he probably wouldn't have time for more than a quick run through.

Jay got to the studio and took a quick look at the score. It wasn't as simple as he had hoped. There were complex harmony lines for the horn section, he had to play the lead melody in and out of commercial breaks, and there was a brief improv section at the top of the show.

He began to panic. How was he going to pull this off? The trombone player noticed Jay's anxiety. Pointing to the score he told Jay, "Don't try to do all that. What of this can you do?"

"Probably just hit a couple of notes cleanly."

"Then just do that."

There are two kinds of confidence. The one we are most familiar with is experi-ential confidence: "The more experience I have the more confidence I feel." Experiential confidence can also be defined as, "I feel more confident when I am having a better experience." When we do well early on in a performance, we can ride a wave of confidence. Also, if we're in the middle of a difficult performance and something happens that shifts the momentum (e.g., positive crowd response) in our favor, we use that shift to gain confidence. But if that momentum shift doesn't happen, we can prematurely conclude that this wasn't our day and submit to our fears and frustrations. Experiential confidence is limited by factors we cannot control. The more our confidence is reliant on those uncertain factors, the more insecure we are, and the more we will turn to over-control and avoidance as a way of coping. Basing our confidence on the amount we have prepared or experienced is a form of over-control. When we only rely on experiential confidence, fear becomes overwhelming in unex-pected or uncertain scenarios like Jay's example. That is why performers will often use superstitious rituals to feel more in control.

While experiential confidence isn't a bad thing, it is limited. There is another type of confidence that can be utilized to avoid the pitfalls of experiential confidence, volitional confidence. Volitional confidence is confidence by choice. It essentially means, "When I feel that I can't, what of this CAN I do?" Volitional confidence can help counteract fear-based coping patterns. Focusing on "What of this can I do" bypasses reliance on preparation. For someone who copes with fear through over-control and over-preparation, choosing to work with what you have in situations where you are unable to prepare can move you beyond your neurological patterns to a place of flow. Additionally, for those who are prone to coping with fear through avoidance and procrastination, focusing on "What of this can I do" breaks the task down to approachable portions. There are many situations when we intend to spend time on an important project but find ourselves avoiding that work out of fear or discomfort. When the time comes to do the work, we begin thinking of ways to avoid having to step into that hard work. At that moment when we feel the pull of "can't", we can say, "What of this CAN I do at this time?" Even if the answer is, "I can work on this for 10 minutes," it moves us beyond our neurological patterns to a place of productivity. Whenever our behavior follows "can't", we give more power to the motivational pull of fear and comfort. Whenever we step into "can", no matter how small a step it is, we lead with values and it starts to change how we process fear (Greenberg, 2017; Schwartz & Beyette, 1997; Schwartz & Begley, 2002; Schwartz, Stapp, & Beauregard, 2004; Schwartz, 2011).

Strategy #5: Moving from striving for passion, happiness, potential, and balance to striving for purpose, meaning, expression, and harmony

"Just do what makes you happy and reach for your potential," Stephanie's parents used to say. Words that had guided Stephanie through her young life. However, now she was at the end of another 70-hour working week and dreading having to start it all over again on Monday. Stephanie was certainly not feeling the joy of working in an art gallery. A career in art had always been her passion. A balance of life and work that she thought would make her happy. But there wasn't any balance in being her boss's punching bag twelve hours a day. Running around town to fill her boss's allergy prescription certainly didn't feel like 'reaching her potential.' What did that even mean? Now, two years into paying her dues, she questioned whether she had followed the right path.

How many times have you heard the importance of pursuing your passion, striving to do what makes you happy, reaching for your potential, or balancing life and work? They are wonderful concepts. They also get in our way because they pull fear to the foreground. Living with passion and happiness causes us to become highly sensitive to how we're feeling. But emotions can be affected by many factors beyond our control. If we're constantly striving for passion and happiness, what happens if we go through a couple of weeks of not feeling either? Two responses tend to happen that work against us. First, we can become very evaluative and start questioning whether we're doing the right thing. Second, we can put pressure on ourselves to search for something that will help us feel better as soon as possible, which may or may not be healthy or congruent with our values.

The same problem occurs with the concepts of striving for our potential and work/life balance. Striving for potential is supposed to motivate us. Striving for work/life balance is supposed to keep us healthy. Neither are very effective in accomplishing those goals. Potential is actually a false concept founded in fear and mistrust. While it's a wonderful cliché, it's based on the premise that you must constantly be reaching for something unattainable in order to motivate yourself to act. The concept of potential represents a mistrust in your ability to self-motivate. The demand for potential is intended to be a pep talk to get us to move. The problem is that it actually can make us more passive because we know that reaching our potential is not possible. If we're demanding ourselves to reach our potential, and say we have four important roles in our life (education, relationships, art, health), then we're demanding 400% energy with only 100% to give. We're always falling short. And the notion that shooting beyond our reach is motivational misleads us to chronically evaluate whether we're reaching our potential or not, which can foster more insecurity. We know we're trying to fool ourselves to strive for perfection, but using tricks to self-motivate fosters mistrust in ourselves which elevates fear.

Work/life balance is another concept that eventually works against us. The intention is to be attentive to our overall wellbeing and not over-invest our identity in our work. It's a motivational strategy. Unfortunately, it can lead to frustration and resentment. Most of us live in a world where our demands exceed our resources of time and energy, making it impossible to attain a true level of work/life balance. So, when we strive for work/life balance, we become very sensitive to how unbalanced we are. We can judge ourselves negatively for not feeling balanced or become resentful of the world that won't allow it. So, again, we set a standard that we fear we can't attain and judge ourselves harshly when we fall short.

What is a different approach that keeps fear in its sweet spot and keeps values in the foreground? Instead of striving for passion and happiness, strive for purpose and meaning. For many, purpose and meaning connote the same thing. For others, purpose has more of a motivational dimension and meaning has more of a reflective dimension. If I strive for purpose, I bring my values into the foreground of my thinking without demanding any emotion like passion to be attached to it. There are many things we do that we don't like but have purpose for us. On days when acting on purpose brings good feelings with it like passion, then that's an added bonus, not the determining factor of whether we're engaged in something right for us. Similarly, if I become more focused on finding meaning in the day rather than happiness, I am focusing on something deeper than just my current mood or emotion. I'm bringing my values into play by reflecting on activities that were meaningful to me. On days when that reflection also makes me happy, it's another bonus, but not the new standard.

Instead of striving for potential, strive for expression. Striving for expression of your values is something we can control and draws energy from our values relationship rather than from motivational tricks. Fear stays in the background and values lead. Challenges transition from being fear triggers to just a reality of living a life of purpose and meaning.

Instead of striving for balance, strive for harmony. At the beginning of each day, decide what you believe is the right devotion of your time and energy in relation to your life roles. You may feel that the right thing for you to do is to spend 90 percent of your time on one role, 5 percent on another, and 5 percent on another. The next day, wipe the slate clean and ask the same question. The answer may be the same or completely different. Sometimes you may only be able to spend 2 percent of your time once a week, on an important life role. That may not seem balanced, but you are harmonizing your values with other important components of your life. If each day you are prioritizing your time and energy according to what you believe is most right, you are living in harmony with your values. If an orchestra strived to play in a balanced manner, the sound wouldn't capture the contrasts of each instrument nor movements of the music.

Paradoxically, the more you strive for purpose, meaning, expression, and harmony, the more you experience passion, happiness, balance and optimal performance. It's attaining these experiences by effect instead of intention.

Strategy #6: Moving from perceiving outcomes as life-critical "have to"s to life-enhancing "want to"s

Alan had to do well in pre-med to pursue his dream of becoming a doctor. Now he had to pass the MCAT. People assumed that to become a doctor you had to do well in pre-med, hunker down in grad school, and then survive residency. But the MCAT was vital. Imagine if he didn't pass. That was not an option.

Grad school was difficult, but he had to do well. He endured the labs, the classes, the memorization. Then it was time for residency.

Residency was insane. 90 hour weeks. No sleep. Impossible scenarios. Residency was designed to be absurdly hard and Alan certainly felt at times like he was going to break. "I have to get through this."

A motorcycle accident victim was rushed into the ER in a critical condition. The Chief Resident assigned Alan to lead the emergency operation. Alan was relatively focused, but couldn't help thinking, "I have to save this man's life."

Alan exhibited proficiency but struggled to commit to a strategy. Eventually, the doctor had to step in and take over the procedure. The patient survived, but Alan considered his performance a failure. "I have to do better." A nurse who had assisted in the surgery pulled Alan aside. "You felt like you had to save him, right?"

"Of course I did."

"When you feel like you have to do something, you significantly impair your critical and creative thinking. I know it's tough when a life is on the line, but 'have-to' works against you."

We all know that outcomes are important. Outcomes serve five positive purposes: (1) they can serve as an additional motivation to do something we find hard, unpleasant, or boring; (2) they serve as a reward for our hard work; (3) they provide feedback about our work; (4) they can create expanded opportunities for us in the future; and (5) we tend to feel positively evaluated by others when we attain outcomes. So, outcomes matter a lot. It's okay to want positive outcomes. And as long as outcomes remain a "want to" in our mental approach, they work for us. However, when outcomes shift from a "want to" to a "have to", they significantly get in the way of our optimal performance. If I have to have an outcome, then I cannot fail. If I cannot fail, then my fear of failure exponentially increases and I can slip into over-control or avoidance mode, resulting in a plateau effect.

How do we keep outcomes in perspective amidst the pressure of needing outcomes to succeed in life? The key is to move from a noun focus to a verb focus. Nouns are outcomes (e.g., grades, achievements, relationships), which we don't completely control. When we have the mindset of needing outcomes, we are very noun-focused. By contrast, verbs are what we do. They are our actions, which we have more control over. When we don't control something, we become more aware of uncertainty, which can increase fear. A verb focus keeps fear in perspective because it concentrates our energy and attention on our behavior instead of factors beyond our control.

In fact, you can limit your focus to just four verbs each day: *learning, expressing what you've learned, relating,* and *taking care of yourself.* At any given time of the day, one of these fours verbs will be relevant. When you study, study to learn, not for grades. When it's time to take a test, focus on expressing what you've learned. When interacting with others, focus on how you want to relate with the other person (e.g., with kindness, curiosity, respect). When we focus on the relationship instead of relating, we become very evaluative and constantly read how the other person is reacting to us. Concentrating on the verb of relating is one of the skills people with social anxiety use to interact more effectively with others despite feeling uncomfortable. And any time during the day when you're not learning, expressing what you've learned, or relating, focus on taking care of yourself. Whenever you find yourself overwhelmed by nouns and outcomes, take a deep breath, and move into the most applicable verb.

There are several advantages to being verb-focused. First, it keeps fear in its proper perspective. Second, the more verb-focused you are, the more nouns you collect. You actually attain more outcomes because you're in an optimal mindset for high performance. There's a popular mantra about the importance of focusing on process versus outcome for high performance. That's partly true. It's not just process, though; it has to be purposeful process. You must be engaged in a process that has true purpose and relevance for you in order to perform at your highest level. A third advantage is that hard work is more acceptable when you're verb-focused. When you're staying within yourself and engaged in purposeful work, you are more accepting of the hardness and stress that comes with it. When we're focused on nouns, we become overwhelmed with everything we have to control to get the outcomes. The difficulty of all we have to attend to and manage becomes less acceptable. Fourth, and most important, when we are verb-focused, we experience more joy when we actually attain outcomes. When we have to have an outcome and are noun-focused, the first emotion we experience when we attain that outcome is not joy, it's relief. When we're verb-focused, the success is in the work and outcomes are viewed as a bonus, the icing on the cake. Remember, there is nothing wrong with wanting an outcome, it's needing it that gets in our way.

We work with students, like Alan in the example, who feel they have to attain a certain Grade Point Average in order to stay on track in competitive career paths. When these students state their outcome goal as needing an A, we ask them to make a list of everything that has to happen for them to get an A in that particular class. Then we ask them to cross off everything that they don't control. The listed items left over are what we call Positioning Goals. These are items that are within their control and best position them to get an A. Positioning Goals should be the primary focus. Giving attention to the other items on the list distracts from Positioning Goals and can negatively impact performance. Try this exercise the next time you feel a strong need for a particular outcome.

Key points

1. There is a dynamic relationship between values and fear because of the uncertainty that surrounds what is important to us. When we flourish, we are not less afraid, we hold fear well. The key is to lead with your values and have fear follow. Here are six strategies that help keep fear of failure in the proper perspective:
    a. Strategy #1: Moving from perceiving fear as an emotion of threat to an **emotion of importance**.
    b. Strategy #2: Moving from perceiving failure as a personal statement to an **experience of worthy disappointment**.
    c. Strategy #3: Moving from perceiving hurt as awful (requiring protection) to **viewing hurt only as difficult**.
    d. Strategy #4: Shifting from experiential confidence to **volitional confidence**.

    e. Strategy #5: Moving from striving for passion, happiness, potential, and balance to **striving for purpose, meaning, expression, and harmony**.

    f. Strategy #6: Moving from perceiving outcomes as life-critical "have to"s to **life-enhancing "want to"s**.

2. To keep outcomes in perspective, shift from being noun-focused to verb-focused. A parent at one of our workshops came up with the following acronym to remember the four optimal verbs: ALERT. Actions, staying verb-focused; Learning; Expressing what you've learned and your abilities to date; Relating; and Taking care of yourself.

3. The more verb-focused we are, the more nouns we collect and the more joy we experience.

Personalizing the concepts

1. From the six strategies, pick one that feels most relevant to you at this time in your life. What are the reasons why this particular strategy resonates with you now? Make an effort to be more mindful of this strategy as you approach each day. Later on, in Chapter 11, you will add this strategy to your final blueprint.

References

Gentile, M.C. (2010). *Giving voice to values: How to speak your mind when you know what's right.* New Haven, CT: Yale University Press.

Greenberg, M. (2017). *The stress-proof brain: Master your emotional response to stress using mindfulness & neuroplasticity.* Oakland, CA: New Harbinger.

Schwartz, J.M., & Beyette, B. (1997). *Brain lock: Free yourself from obsessive-compulsive behavior.* New York: Regan Books.

Schwartz, J.M., & Begley, S. (2002). *The mind and the brain: Neuroplasticity and the power of the mental force.* New York: Regan Books.

Schwartz, J.M., Stapp, H.P., and Beauregard, M. (2004). The volitional influence of the mind on the brain, with special reference to emotional self-regulation. In Beauregard, M. (Ed.), *Consciousness, emotional self-regulation, and the brain* (pp. 195–238). Philadelphia, PA: John Benjamins.

Schwartz, J.M. (2011). *You are not your brain: The 4-step solution for changing bad habits, ending unhealthy thinking, and taking control of your life.* New York: Avery.

Notes

9 Paradigm Shift 4

Shifting from avoidance of difficult emotions to confidence in managing difficult emotions

When Laura was an intern at an esteemed literary agency, she worked to prove herself worthy of a permanent job. When she became an agent's assistant, she worked to prove that she deserved the job. Reading query letters and working with authors were the only aspects of the job that saved her from overwhelming stress. "I need to prove myself to the other agents."

After three years, Laura had matured into a rising star within the agency. She wasn't a full-time agent, but she had a few clients of her own and was assisting one of the partnering agents. More importantly, Laura had learned not to further complicate busy weeks or large projects by imposing expectations on herself.

This month in particular was a busy month. Her boss was out of the country to focus on international distribution and a big-name author was having a crisis with her publisher. When the partnering agent returned, he was impressed by how well Laura had put out fires and managed his clients. The agent recommended to the other partners that Laura be promoted to a full-time agent.

Shortly after the recommendation, Laura happened to overhear a managing partner talking to another partner. The managing partner, who was male, said to the other partner, who was also male, "I can't make Laura a full-time agent. She's too sexy. Can you imagine working with her all the time? She'd probably take a joke the wrong way and sue me."

The hurt and anger Laura felt was staggering. She had worked so hard and accomplished so much for the agency. She had built meaningful relationships with writers and publishers. This unacceptable misogyny was what had been holding her back?

Laura reached out to a friend at the agency to brainstorm ways to address the problem without jeopardizing her career. However, she struggled to act on her options through a cloud of hurt and anger.

One afternoon, Laura talked to one of her authors about some publishing logistics, and afterwards they got on to the topic of ideas for the author's new book. Laura fell into the conversation, inspired by the author's ideas. The conversation quickly lasted two hours. The author told Laura that she was a great agent because she cared about the work. Laura was reminded of how much she loved being a part of important concepts and getting those works produced. That's what mattered to her.

Laura decided to start pulling her resumé together and put out feelers to other agencies. She was not going to put her fear of job security ahead of what she loved about her career. Before leaving the agency or filing a complaint with HR, Laura decided to address the issue with the managing partner who had made the sexist comments.

"John, I've worked very hard for this agency for over three years now. I've developed authors, sold manuscripts, put out fires ... done good work that has enhanced this company's value."

"I agree."

"I feel that I should've been promoted to a full-time agent by now, but I have been held back for reasons that have nothing to do with work."

"I thought a couple of agents would have moved on by now ... You're young, but I always planned on promoting you."

"John, I overheard you and Dale talking ... and you said some pretty inappropriate ... sexist comments about me."

"What did I say?"

"You described my appearance as a reason to avoid promoting me. Aside from the implication that you've intentionally inhibited my career, it is not acceptable to talk about another coworker's appearance."

"I was just joking around with Dale. I didn't mean any of it."

"It is not acceptable to talk about an employee's appearance in any manner."

"It was a joke. No one can take a joke these days. You don't think I was razzed when I was coming up?"

The managing partner continued to downplay the incident. Laura focused on her love of developing authors and selling book proposals, rather than letting the fear of losing her job dissuade her from reporting the managing partner. He had not been responsive or willing to learn when she addressed the issue, so Laura decided to move forward in reporting him to HR. She was nervous about how her decision would affect her career, but trusted that she was a good agent who cared about the work regardless of the challenges surrounding her.

In the training so far, you have acquired a richer understanding of your values. You have practiced making values your primary motivator by developing an active relationship with your values. You have clarified healthy and unhealthy boundaries of your values in action. And you have learned ways to manage fear differently so that your values lead in your decision-making and behavior. This hard work moves you toward a more consistent level of productivity, fulfillment, and resilience. However, being engaged with your values means that you are also opening yourself up to significant stress and difficult emotions. Furthermore, despite doing all we can to flourish, we will also experience disappointment and loss from factors we can't control. How do we thrive through significant stress, difficult emotions, disappointment, or heartbreak? How do we cope effectively when we are managing something upsetting in our lives that we can't fix or influence?

The toughest emotions to manage are hurt, worry, guilt, anger, and at times, boredom. Stress is a psychological reaction to those difficult emotions. We don't desire these emotions and they always seem to take longer to recover from than we would prefer. However, when we flourish, we are less concerned about reducing difficult emotions through over-control and avoidance, and more focused on managing strong emotions in a healthy manner. This chapter describes principles for coping and self-care that develop a greater confidence in managing difficult emotions. The more confident we are in our ability to manage stress and strong emotions, the less over-protective or evasive we will be around emotions such as hurt. If I know I can manage hurt in a healthy manner, then I won't fear it as much. This allows me to lead with my values.

There are extensive educational resources that focus on specific strategies and techniques for stress and emotional management (David, 2016; Greenberg, 2017; Hayes, Follette, & Linehan, 2004; Hayes & Smith, 2005; Kabat-Zinn, 1990; Lehrer, Woolfolk, & Sime; 2008; Linehan, 2014; Meichenbaum, 1985; Subramanian, 2001). This chapter will focus less on specific strategies and more on the processes we've found to be common among those who flourish through difficult times. In fact, most people who thrive through hardship have a very distilled process of self-management that is not laden with a complex array of strategies and techniques. Their approach is very basic, but intentional and effective. They focus on a few key principles and stay engaged in life, despite its current difficulties.

Before we look at ways to process difficult emotions, we're going to analyze why our values can leave us vulnerable to difficult emotions and consequent stress.

Stress and values

Stress within roles

You may be experiencing stress because the values you want fulfilled in a certain life role (work, education, relationships, leisure, etc.) are not being rewarded. The environment or people in authority may be preventing you from fulfilling your values or demanding that you spend time and energy on other values. Relief from this stress can occur if you try to redefine your responsibilities in that role, develop other activities that will compensate and allow for the values to be satisfied, or leave that environment.

Stress between roles

You may be experiencing stress because the time and energy you are spending on one life role is interfering with the time you can devote to roles where other values are being fulfilled. The challenge with this type of stress is to accept the importance of reprioritizing your time and energy according to your values.

Unfortunately, this is an exercise people often do after a tragedy puts life into perspective; you don't have to wait for that to happen. Use your LVI results as a starting point for prioritizing your time and gradually start making the changes at a rate that feels realistic for you.

Stress of managing too many values

You may experience stress because you are trying to manage too many values that feel critical but are unable to attend to most of them particularly well. Many lifestyles do not permit people to satisfy a large number of values. Relief from this stress comes from a very difficult shift in mindset: a true acceptance that there are only so many hours in a day and that the rigid demand you are placing on yourself is actually getting in the way of fulfilling your values. Reduce your list of critical values to a number that feels possible with the time and energy you currently have. You can change this list as your time and energy allow. It takes courage to prioritize because it is difficult to manage two or more "right" decisions. Out of fear we can say yes to several "right" decisions, which can lead to over-commitment. Sometimes we freeze and wait until we have to jump to a decision. Sometimes we land in a good place, sometimes we don't. A healthy relationship with our values honors courageous prioritization: "In this situation, I will choose this value to act on." When we approach this choice as an opportunity to learn, rather than needing to make the right decision, we become more adept at prioritizing our values in accordance with realistic understandings of our time and energy.

Internal conflict

At times our values can be contradictory and cause ambivalence. For instance, someone who values Belonging and Independence will have to manage the stress of attending to both differing values. Unresolved emotions from difficult life experiences may also interfere with values fulfillment. For example, unresolved fear of failure can interfere with Achievement, and unresolved hurt from broken trust can interfere with Belonging. Being unable to act on values that are important to us can be a sign that our typical methods of coping and support are not enough to work through an important conflict.

Unresolved emotional issues can also cause values to drift into intense needs. When a value becomes a need, the fulfillment we feel from expressing that value starts to be replaced with stress and intensity. This is because we are over-attending to that need at the expense of other important values. For example, if you value Responsibility you will be motivated to be dependable and trustworthy. But needing to be responsible is overwhelming because you have to be seen as dependable to everyone in all situations, a need that can never be completely satisfied. You will live in fear of letting others down, and may become stressed to the point where you have no energy for other values. Eventually, the need to be responsible to others results in less responsibility to your own health. It is important to recognize this pattern, to understand how this value became so intense and is negatively impacting your life, and slowly begin the process of putting that value in a healthier perspective. Courageously and gradually devoting more time to another important value can help realign values that have become needs.

It may be helpful to receive additional emotional support because it will feel unsettling and fearful to devote less time to a value that has drifted into a need state. The adjustment will feel wrong at first and may cause guilt. Instead, perceive it as devoting less time to a value in order to experience healthy and fulfilling expressions of that value. For example, if you have over-attended to the Responsibility value and believe it is healthy to devote less time to it, you may initially feel like you're being "irresponsible". Instead, view it as being *optimally* responsible.

Anger

Stress is a psychological response to dealing with difficult emotions. Before we look into principles that can help process difficult emotions, let's look at a particular emotion many of us struggle to manage: anger.

Anger is a secondary emotion. It's not a primary emotion. Four things drive anger: your values (you can't be angry about something that's not important to you), hurt, fear, and fatigue. When you're angry, something has happened that violated something important to you (values). You may be upset about that violation (hurt). You may be worried about the implications of that violation (fear). You may be tired of experiencing that type of violation, or you may be generally exhausted so your tolerance for minor violations is low (fatigue). These four factors can move us into anger mode.

Anger is a protective emotion. We move into anger because it's energizing and safe in the nobility of our rightness. We can stay in that mode for a long time, but eventually it starts to get in our way. It's human to seek the protection of anger when you feel something important has been violated. It's harder to stay at the primary level of values, hurt, fear, and fatigue. When we commit to staying at that level instead of getting angry, we are more capable of participating in conflict resolution and/or coping directly. However, it is very difficult to stay at that primary level because we are vulnerable and don't know what's going to happen. It can help to think of staying at this vulnerable level for the sake of our health. Although anger can be noble, safe, and energizing, it can have negative effects on our physical and mental health. So out of self-care we can choose to courageously move from that anger because it hurts us.

These concepts mainly apply to chronic anger. Temporary anger can be okay: "It feels good to be angry at you right now." However, even short-lived anger only works temporarily; eventually it will also begin to strain us. It's important to process the hurt, fear, and fatigue that sparks the anger.

Processing principles for difficult emotions

Often, effective stress and emotional management depend less on the things you do and more on the order in which you process them. Following these principles can help you gain greater confidence in managing stress and difficult emotions.

1. **Acceptance—seeing stress as a good thing.** *Ask yourself if the current stress you feel is acceptable. If it is, go with it.* Stress itself is not bad. Stress is a function of caring, of importance. It's impossible to be stressed about something that isn't important to you. Stress reduction can be misleading because it may require lowering the importance of something that matters to you. To be engaged in our values means we are also signing up for stress. This is a good thing... up to a point. There is an optimal point where we are engaged in our values but haven't moved them into a need state. For instance, we often go through crunch periods of absurd busyness. If we know that the stress stems from reasons of value and importance, and that the busyness is temporary, we are more likely to find an optimal level of acceptable stress. It is during these crunch times when we need to be more accepting, not evaluative or judgmental. It can also help to keep self-care practices in place even if we only have sparing moments to devote to self-care. The goal is stress management through acceptance, not stress reduction.

2. **Problem-solving.** *If the stress level is not acceptable, ask yourself if there is anything you can do to fix or influence the situation.* There is nothing wrong with moving into "fix it" mode when you're feeling too much stress. There might be a solution. Use your analytical mind, reach out to others for their opinions, and if you find a solution, act on it. However, it's important to keep the objective within your control. It has to be the process of acting that manages the stress, not whether the outcome works out well. For instance, if you have an argument with a friend, one solution is to go and talk things out with him or her. The action of trying to work things out has to be enough, not whether you walk away from the discussion having repaired the relationship because you don't completely control that. If your stress management depends on solutions you don't control, you will set yourself up for more stress if the solutions don't work out the way you want.

3. **Self-imposed pressure.** *If you still feel stressed beyond an acceptable level and have done problem-solving steps that are within your control, ask yourself "Are there any self-imposed pressures or perceptions I am adding to this stress?"* Stress can be exasperated by our perceived demands and perceived capabilities. When our perceived demands exceed our perceived capabilities, we are stressed. At times our thoughts and demands add weight to our stress, making it overwhelming, especially if our perceptions rigidly demand "shoulds" or "needs". For example, "Life should be fair."

"People should treat me with respect and kindness." "There should be equitable return on my effort and care." "I need to achieve this outcome to feel good about myself."

Other forms of self-imposed pressure include over-projecting into the future, making broad conclusions about yourself or others, and seeing everything around you as critically important and trying to over-control as a way of managing fear.

Become more aware of the pressures you are demanding of yourself and whether they are motivational or getting in the way. When you feel over-stressed and notice that it's because of a self-imposed pressure, tell yourself to "Stop. These thoughts are normal, but they're not helping me right now. What's one thing I can focus on doing right now that I believe would be healthy?" This helps you catch, recover, and gradually replace inhibiting thought patterns with more helpful ones.

4. **Effective coping.** *If you still feel stressed beyond an acceptable level, if you have attempted problem-solving steps that are within your control, and you are managing your own self-imposed pressures, then your task is coping.* To develop confidence in managing the harshness that is sometimes our life experience, people who flourish focus primarily on three essential steps. The good news is that these steps are easy to understand and apply. The bad news is that they are unnatural and tend to be the opposite to how we respond to loss, disappointment, and stress.

Coping Step 1: Honor the reaction, challenge any conclusions

When we're going through a difficult time, the most natural reaction is to try and distance ourselves from the hurt and disappointment. We tend to move toward any soothing behavior that will calm the intensity of the harsh emotion. During this time, we also tend to get very conclusive about ourselves, our future, and the world around us. "See, you can't trust anyone." "Well, there goes my dream job." We can cope effectively when we reverse this process. We honor the reaction and affirm that we're upset because something upsetting has happened. We realize that our reaction is valid and that we have come by it honestly. Instead of working so hard to distance ourselves from the emotion, we focus our work on another task: challenging any conclusions. When we are reacting to something upsetting, our most typical reaction is to ruminate on **three** questions:

- What does this say about *me*?
- What does this say about *the world around me*?
- What does this say about *my future*?

These three questions only intensify and stall the storm because the answers will be filtered through our current emotional state. The work is to catch ourselves when we make statements about ourselves, our future, or our world, and move into a healthier focus: "What's something I can do to take care of myself during this difficult time?"

Coping Step 2: Commit to self-care for the health of it (not to feel better)

When our focus shifts from conclusions to self-care, it is important that we distinguish self-care from soothing. When we seek to soothe, our intention is to feel better, to change our mood. The quickest and most potent methods to change our brain chemistry (i.e., mood) are through food, drugs, pain/exercise, sex, or compelling entertainment (e.g., movies, TV, gaming, shopping). We tend not to moderate these soothing methods well. We can also develop a sense of entitlement about soothing behavior. "I deserve this food." "I deserve this drink." "I deserve this [activity] that will make me feel better." Striving to soothe pushes us into a need state instead of a recovery state. When we "need" to feel better, that becomes the primary guide of our behavior and decision-making, and it is rarely healthy. We begin to cope effectively when we shift our focus from feeling better to healthy behavior. As in Coping Step 1, when you commit to honoring your reaction, you don't have to rush to distance yourself from the pain but you will want some action to assist in holding the difficult emotions. While there are a lot of ways to soothe, there are few healthy ways to take care of yourself when you're upset.

> *Verbal expression and social support.* Talking with someone we trust is a healthy form of self-care. Some can view verbal expression as utilitarian or ineffective. "What good does it do to talk about something if it doesn't change anything?" But, sometimes the process of venting to someone we trust helps us tolerate our distress. Receiving support from others is healthy and not a threat to our self-sufficiency. Sometimes the most independent thing we can do is to utilize the supportive resources around us. Support doesn't only mean emotional support. There are eight dimensions of social support that will be described later in this chapter.
>
> *Physical expression.* Converting our emotional energy to physical expression can be a helpful form of coping. This can include exercise and physical activity, athletics, progressive muscle relaxation, active breathing exercises, yoga, etc. It doesn't mean we have to be in an emotional state while we're exercising or that the activity has to be congruent with the emotion (e.g., boxing and anger). Dedicating physical activity in part to the difficult emotions we are holding helps us process and cope.
>
> *Creative expression.* Converting our emotional energy to some form of creative expression is a helpful form of self-care. Any form of creative expression, such as writing, artwork, music, whether or not we are skilled at it, can help us cope. Make a note of any training that you may be interested in exploring with any of these self-care

practices. For example, taking acting classes, painting workshops, music lessons, etc. can be healthy activities for self-care.

Meditative expression. Meditative and spiritual forms of expression or reflection are calming practices of emotional management. This self-care option can foster acceptance of our current state and the temporary nature of challenging emotions. Examples are mindfulness exercises, meditation, prayer, guided imagery, etc.

Temporary break. Taking a temporary reprieve from your stress through distraction can be healthy. There is a difference between suppressing an emotion and temporarily setting an emotion to one side. The latter acknowledges that you are aware something is affecting you but you want a temporary break from it. Examples are watching TV, reading, hanging out with friends, attending an event, or working. Distraction should not be the only self-care practice you have, but it is periodically healthy.

What else is true? When we are coping with an emotional storm, we tend to see everything through our emotional filter. For example, if we are angry with someone, it is hard to see that person from a perspective other than what they did to make us angry. Reminding ourselves that there is a broader reality to our current emotion and identifying specific things about our life and our world that are also true can help us cope.

Appropriate inappropriateness. There are times when it is healthy to express our objection to the difficulty or pain of our current reality. "I can accept it, but I don't have to like it." Finding small ways to protest, rebel, or laugh at the absurdity of our situation can help us cope, but requires management so that it doesn't hurt ourselves or others.

Dreaming. We can't control this form of self-care, but dreaming can be a healthy form of emotional processing. The next time you remember a dream, try to recall the most prominent emotions in the dream; they will often relate to the emotions you are currently working through or processing.

It is important not to practice these forms of self-care with the intent of feeling better. We will often drop healthy self-care practices because we don't feel better after doing them. However, those practices are exactly what will help us cope and recover even though we don't immediately feel positive effects. Abandoning healthy practices is especially common with activities that used to make us feel good, but aren't viscerally helping us during periods of distress. Recovery rarely occurs at the pace we prefer. Self-care practices serve as a slight wind to move emotional storms along. We have to hang in there, respect the pace, and commit to self-care activities because of their coping power, not because of how they immediately make us feel.

Coping Step 3: Do something of personal rightness (focus on a value while affected)

Finally, after respecting that we are affected and devoting time to self-care, we need to do something each day that is congruent with our values. Whether we emotionally find meaning in it or not, we can recover when we believe that we are still engaged in life in a way that corresponds with our values. No matter how bad or awful we feel, we can always do something, even for a minute, that is in line with a value we find or have found important. It's critical to show yourself that you can stay engaged in life when you may be deeply affected by a life experience. It can help to revisit your LVI profile or the healthy/unhealthy expressions of your values that you listed in Chapter 7 (Paradigm Shift 2). Each day, focus on a particular value that feels true and honest to you. Even if the best effort you can give is 10 percent of your expression, step into it. It's imperative, when we're deeply affected, to demonstrate to ourselves that we can be affected by something without being defined by it. Focusing on a value and acting on it keeps us defined by our authenticity, rather than our hurt.

Coping Step 3 is especially important when we are grieving a distinct loss or when we are experiencing something systemic in our environment that is a values violation. A values violation is when we experience something that feels fundamentally wrong to us. Both loss and violation bring with them more than hurt. Fear joins with this hurt as we are compelled to think about the future implications and meaning of the violation. It's most natural for us to become intensely focused on the loss and violation to the point where our actions and behavior can become primarily guided by the hurt. While this pattern is completely normal, it's unsustainable and depleting. At some point in time, we have to turn our focus from the values violation to the values, from our loss to our meaning. By focusing on a value and acting on it, even if it's a little at a time, day after day, we can move toward recovery and a growing confidence in coping with values violations that we may repeatedly experience.

Coping and social support

As mentioned in the *verbal expression* self-care practice, there are eight dimensions of social support (Hardy & Crace, 1993; Hardy, Burke, & Crace, 2005). Very rarely will one person be able to adequately provide all the dimensions of social support. So, it is important to develop a social support network of people we can count on for the multiple dimensions of our challenges.

Listening: Someone who actively listens without giving advice or being judgmental.

Emotional support: Someone you trust who provides comfort, care, and encouragement.

Emotional challenge: Someone who challenges you to examine your perspective, values, thoughts, and feelings.

Task appreciation: Someone who acknowledges your efforts and expresses
appreciation for your work.

Task challenge: Someone who challenges the way you think about a
task or activity that can lead to greater creativity, motivation, and
involvement.

Reality confirmation: Someone who is coming from a similar reality or
context, and helps confirm your perspective of the world.

Tangible assistance: Someone who provides financial assistance, products,
and/or gifts.

Personal assistance: Someone who provides services or help through the
contribution of their time and energy.

Conclusions

Fortunately, these principles of emotional management are complementary.
For example, we can be more accepting of our experience when we focus on
self-care practices, and we can better problem-solve when we manage our self-
imposed pressures.

Once an emotional storm has passed to the point where we believe we have
a healthy perspective, it can be a good time to reflect and find meaning in the
experience that may help us to facilitate growth and confidence in managing
difficult emotions in the future.

Key points

1. Values-based living leaves us vulnerable to difficult emotions such as
   hurt, anger, and worry. Stress is a psychological response to those tough
   emotions. Instead of working toward stress reduction through avoidance
   or over-control, we can become more resilient by developing confidence
   in our ability to manage difficult emotions in a healthy way.
2. The order in which we process challenging emotions can lead to more
   effective stress and emotional management.
   a. Stress is not itself bad. It is a sign of importance. If you're experien-
      cing an acceptable amount of challenging stress, go with it.
   b. If the stress is at an unacceptable level, see if there is anything you
      can do to fix or influence the situation. Remember, it is the act of
      problem-solving that manages the stress and not the result, which is
      determinate on factors beyond your control.
   c. If you have tried to problem-solve and the level of stress is still
      unacceptable, check to see if there are any self-imposed pressures
      expounding the stress.
   d. When difficult emotions are still overwhelming, the task is coping.
      Focus on the Three Effective Coping Steps: (1) honor your reaction,

and challenge any conclusions; (2) commit to self-care for the health of it, not to feel better; and (3) do something of personal rightness by focusing on a value while you are affected.

3. It is helpful to develop a social support network when coping with the multiple dimensions of our challenges.

Personalizing the concepts

1. Pick one Effective Coping Step that feels most relevant to you at this time in your life. Also, pick one self-care practice that works for you and one that you'd like to try (note any training this may involve, e.g., music lessons). What are the reasons why these particular selections resonate with you now? Make an effort to be more mindful of these choices as you approach each day. Later on, in Chapter 11, you will add these answers to your final blueprint.

References

David, S. (2016). *Emotional agility: Get unstuck, embrace change, and thrive in work and life*. New York: Avery.

Greenberg, M. (2017). *The stress-proof brain: Master your emotional response to stress using mindfulness & neuroplasticity*. Oakland, CA: New Harbinger.

Hardy, C.J., Burke, K.L., & Crace, R.K. (2005). Coaching: An effective communication system. In S. Murphy (Ed.), *The sport psych handbook: A complete guide to today's best mental training techniques* (pp. 191–212). Champaign, IL: Human Kinetics.

Hardy, C.J., & Crace, R.K. (1993). The dimensions of social support when dealing with sport injuries. In D. Pargman (Ed.), *Psychological bases of sport injuries* (pp. 121–144). Morgantown, WV: Fitness Information Technology.

Hayes, S.C., Follette, V.M., & Linehan, M.M. (Eds.) (2004). *Mindfulness and acceptance: Expanding the cognitive-behavioral tradition*. New York: Guilford.

Hayes, S.C., & Smith, S. (2005). *Get out of your mind and into your life: The new acceptance and commitment therapy*. Oakland, CA: New Harbinger.

Kabat-Zinn, J. (1990). *Full catastrophe living: Using the wisdom of your body and mind to face stress, pain and illness*. New York: Delacorte.

Lehrer, P.M., Woolfolk, R.L., & Sime, W.E. (Eds.) (2008). *Principles and practice of stress management* (3rd ed.). New York: Guilford.

Linehan, M.M. (2014). *DBT skills training manual* (2nd ed.). New York: Guilford.

Meichenbaum, D. (1985). *Stress inoculation training*. New York: Prentice-Hall.

Subramanian, S. (2001). Life values and perceived occupational stress among cosmopolitan (scientific) and local (administrative)-oriented scientists in R & D organizations. *Asia Pacific Business Review*, 6(4), 74–81.

Notes

10 Paradigm Shift 5

Shifting from a chronically evaluative mindset to an expressive mindset

Gabe was 28 years old and couldn't swim. After a litany of YouTube videos, library books, and informed conversations, he went to the pool. The Aquatic Center was another world. Tight splashes echoing over the deck; lane lines floating on perfect blue ripples; lap swimmers flowing back and forth. Gabe waded into the shallow end of the slow lane and set off.

A few lanes down Taylor was expertly swimming through his workout. His mind raced as he swam, "Just two more minutes then I'm done with this set, and then two more sets... This is too much. Go back to the office... No, if I don't finish these sets today, then I have to double up tomorrow." Each lap became more daunting. "Finish swimming; work on the proposal till four; meeting till six; research analytics till I'm ready for Friday's pitch; dinner; call Michael; finish up the proposal hopefully before midnight... I'm going so slow. Push it, Taylor! Just two more 100s... then two more sets."

Gabe launched into his maiden voyage. A collision of memorized techniques caused a four-limb pile up. Gabe grabbed hold of a lane line and hoisted himself up. He caught his breath, recalled some training tips, and set off again. His arms obeyed while his legs sank. He flailed forward until his head could not find air. He grabbed the lane line again. EEEEKKK! EEEEKK! The lifeguard blew his whistle and yelled, "You can't hold onto the lane line!"

The clock read 1:14 AM and Taylor still hadn't finished the proposal. He had to call it a night or he wouldn't get up by 5 AM. He lay in bed exhausted but unable to sleep. "What do I have to do to catch up tomorrow? Phone calls, research, finish the proposal, work out... I've got to be better about sticking to my schedule."

That night Gabe encouraged himself, "Ok, good job getting in the water. What did I learn? My legs kept sinking and my motions were sporadic which made me sink faster... Floating! I need to float. One of the videos talked about floating." Gabe looked up floating videos online and imagined how it would feel to float and glide in the water.

After two weeks, Gabe was still grabbing hold of the lane lines, but only occasionally. He was able to float up and down the length of the pool while moving his body in a way that propelled the floating rather than interrupted it.

A few weeks later, Gabe was approaching the Aquatic Center where he saw a man reading a sign taped to the locked door. The man was Taylor. "Of course its closed! S**t! The one hour I have! Today's my swim day."

"Pool's closed?"

"For maintenance. Can you believe that? Don't give us a head's up or any-thing!" Taylor recognized Gabe as the guy who struggled to swim. Gabe recognized Taylor as the proficient swimmer who could seemingly glide half a lap with each stroke.

"Too bad... Hey I've seen you swim. You're really good. Have you been swimming since you were a kid?"

"Yeah, since High School."

"I'm trying to teach myself. Any suggestions?"

"Umm... Yeah... uhh, look I gotta run to another gym and try to squeeze in a workout, but check out this one book, Lap Flow, it explains things better than I can."

"Lap Flow, got it. Thanks."

As Taylor ran to his car he turned back, "Look, I've been swimming my whole life and it's frustrating 'cause you can never perfect it."

"That's what I like about it."

Paradigm Shift 5 presents five training steps you can do every day to develop an expressive mindset. These action steps take about ten minutes a day, and we've found that when people flourish they focus on something like these steps throughout the day in order to train for flow.

Most of us have heard of or experienced a flow state or a zone state. It's an experience that feels like a larger energy joining with your energy where things seem to magically fall into place. When studying people who flourish in areas of performance and athletics, we've found that you can actually develop certain components of flow because when you're in a flow state you are also in an expressive mindset.

Developing an expressive mindset correlates to experiencing flow more frequently. These five daily action steps correspond to aspects of flow (Abuhamdeh & Csikszentmihalyi, 2012; Csikszentmihalyi, 1990). What we've found when working with performers and athletes is that those who flourish regularly practice these psychological factors that nurture flow experience.

Five daily action steps

Step 1: Values-based intentionality

At the beginning of each day, ask yourself "What is the most *right* devotion of my time and energy today?" Not what you want to do, or what you have to do. But what is most *right* for you to do? The word *right* is intended to trigger your values and establish a values-based intentionality at the beginning of your day. "What is most *right* for me to do today?" The answer on one day may involve devoting your attention to a number of varying activities that are important to you. Another day the most *right* devotion of your energy may be a singular focus on an important project that is more stressful than fulfilling. On another day, *right* may mean rest. Whatever the day may call for, the concept of *rightness* is designed to tap into your values relationship. Once you've crystallized what matters for the day, then prioritize them to move to what matters *most*. This will align your higher-energy periods of the day with those activities that are of higher priority. This process doesn't have to be long and structured. It can be short and intuitive while you get ready for your day.

Step 2: Volitional confidence and imagery

After you've established the values-based intentions of your day, there can be uncertainty as to whether you can get it all done. If you feel a twinge of doubt, you're probably right. Reduce any part of Step 1 that feels like too much until you feel a sense of confidence, "I can do this."

Volitional confidence is thinking, "When feeling *can't*, what of this *can* I do?" Once you have an acceptable idea of what you can do that day, imagine doing it. If you don't imagine what you value, you'll imagine what you fear. It is natural to become preoccupied with "what if" factors when envisioning the day. "What if *x* happens?" "What if I don't finish *y*?" When we imagine what we fear, we trigger the Fear-Based Model of Excellence and our responses of over-control and avoidance throughout the day. Imagining what we value and what we *can* do in the context of a day counteracts the natural pull to focus on fear.

Step 3: Engagement with experiential acceptance

Once you have imagined your "can do" list of values-based behaviors, focus on expressing those activities for the rest of the day. The day is about being fully engaged in the expression of your talent and energy with courage and commitment. The kicker is engaging with full acceptance of the experience the day provides.

This step is the most difficult in attaining flow experience because it is hard to accept unplanned occurrences. Oftentimes we plan out one day and end up having to express our energies in an entirely different way for important yet unforeseen reasons. When we have developed a strong sense of daily acceptance, we are able to keep fear of the unforeseen in the background. Engaging in the expression of values and committing to full acceptance of the day's events allows us to be versatile in connecting with our values during unplanned circumstances which sets us up for consistent flourishing.

Step 4: Compassion and appreciation

At some point near the end of the day, spend a couple of minutes appreciating what you did and why. This may sound a little touchy-feely for some, but there is a practical reason for doing this. At the end of the day, we most naturally think of the things that didn't get done and what we need to do tomorrow to make up for it. This negatively affects our motivation and stress levels because it triggers an overly evaluative or judgmental mindset right before we go to bed. We already know what didn't get done. So instead, at the end of the day, it can help to take a couple of minutes to appreciate what we did, which counters the negative effects evaluating or judging our day can have. Appreciating what you did is an act of compassion toward your efforts in encountering the day. Compassion puts our minds in a state of openness and reflection, which allows us to learn how unexpected events provide opportunities for values-congruent behavior (Brown, 2012; Neff, 2011). For instance, we may have planned to devote time to an important project but ended up devoting time to a friend in crisis who unexpectedly called. It is important to appreciate the values that are behind that behavior.

One important requirement of this appreciation strategy is "no 'buts' allowed". It negates the whole benefit of this step if you say, "I worked on this project that had purpose for me, *but* I should have worked on it longer" or "I devoted time to helping others today, *but* I could have been more helpful." This step is not intended to be a baseless self-congratulatory endeavor. Its purpose is to train flourishing on a daily basis. By taking the time to appreciate the courage you exhibited in committing to values-based behavior, you increase your motivation and understanding of how to repeat values-congruent behavior.

The compassion and appreciation step tends to be the most neglected of the five. But it is critical in order to have the right mindset to be effective in the next step.

Step 5: Analysis and reflection

After spending time appreciating what you did during the day, ask yourself, "What is one thing I can learn from today that will help me tomorrow?" The previous step of compassion and appreciation is important because if we are in a place of evaluation and judgment this step becomes too threatening and personal. If we bypass this step, we don't learn. You have to be in a place of compassion and appreciation to objectively learn, which leads to growth and improvement over time.

There's a difference between analysis and evaluation. Analysis is an honest, objective attempt to learn. Evaluation is personal. We process experiences as good or bad, success or failure. This works against us and inhibits growth. For example, we may look back at the day and realize that we fell short of a particular goal. Evaluating our actions may cause us to conclude that we were lazy (or some other negative, personal label). This process only serves to negatively effect our motivation and make us vulnerable to repeating the same behavior.

When we analyze instead of evaluate, we are able to look at a situation, understand the factors that influenced our behavior (e.g., "I took on too much today," "I let fear get in the way," or "Something unanticipated happened that was more important"), and learn from the experience.

After you have appreciated and learned, you can mentally flush out the stress of the day with a clear conscience. This can help you sleep better and fully restore your body and mind.

Key points

1. Developing an expressive mindset correlates to experiencing a flow state more frequently.
2. The five daily action steps for developing an expressive mindset:
   a. *Values-based intentionality*: At the beginning of each day, ask yourself, "What is the most *right* devotion of my time and energy today?"
   b. *Volitional confidence and imagery*: Reduce any part of Step 1 that feels like too much until you feel a sense of confidence, "I can do this." Then imagine doing so.
   c. *Engagement with experiential acceptance*: Fully engage in the expression of your talent and energy with acceptance of the experience the day provides.
   d. *Compassion and Appreciation*: At the end of the day, spend time appreciating what you did and why.
   e. *Analysis and reflection*: Ask yourself, "What is one thing I can learn from today that will help me tomorrow?"

Personalizing the concepts

1. Which of these five steps do you find would be the most challenging to implement in your daily life? Where do those challenges stem from? How can you manage them?
2. Practice these steps, which takes about ten minutes a day, every day for eight weeks. Be aware of any differences involving your mindset and effectiveness.

References

Abuhamdeh, S., & Csikszentmihalyi, M. (2012). The importance of challenge for the enjoyment of intrinsically motivated, goal-directed activities. *Personality and Social Psychology Bulletin*, 38(3), 317–330.

Brown, B. (2012). *Daring greatly: How the courage to be vulnerable transforms the way we live, love, parent, and lead*. New York: Gotham.

Csikszentmihalyi, M. (1990). *Flow: the psychology of optimal experience* (1st ed.). New York: Harper & Row.

Neff, K. (2011). *Self-compassion: The proven power of being kind to yourself*. New York: HarperCollins.

Notes

11 Putting it all together

Dynamic Blueprinting Action Plan

Lloyd decided to run a marathon for a charity group that had a last-minute opening. The problem was that the marathon was in four days and Lloyd had not trained to run long distances. It was a struggle. His lungs and knees simply could not push past the pain after thirteen miles, forcing him to withdraw.

The next year, Lloyd was ready for the marathon. He had followed a gradual training program for six months, and was able to finish the marathon at a respectable pace. Lloyd felt accomplishment in finishing the marathon, but was looking forward to spending more time with his family and career now that he didn't have to train for anything. In fact, at work, he came across a project that ended up leading to a promotion.

Before Lloyd knew it, four months had gone by since the marathon and he hadn't run once. He took his family on a beach vacation. One morning he got up early and went for a run on the beach. He could barely make it three miles before having to turn back.

Later that year, Lloyd ran the marathon for a third time, following the same six-month training program he'd used the previous year. However, after this year's marathon, he decided to incorporate a maintenance training program where he ran varied distances three or four times a week. The family returned to the same beach for vacation the following year. Lloyd went for a morning beach run and blew by the previous year's problematic three-mile mark.

It is easy to believe that once we learn new concepts, the new knowledge we have gained should lead to consistent positive change. It takes more to truly internalize new concepts. We have to go through a period of intentionality about these concepts to adapt our mind and body to new ways of thinking. But, as with physical training, if you consistently work on a mental training program that you trust to be credible, your mind will adapt and internalize the concepts. However, as in the same analogy above, if you drift away from your training, this relentless world of change, uncertainty, and pace will result in the return of old habits of living at your neurology. So, the process of mental training for flourishing includes a period of commitment to careful attention (cognitive strain, as discussed in Chapter 7) to the concepts until they become internalized and a natural part of your thinking (cognitive ease). Maintenance training to retain the expressive mindset includes periodic careful attention (cognitive strain). This chapter provides a training plan that is designed for an optimal combination of intentionality and full engagement in your life without being constantly evaluative.

While we have distilled the components of Authentic Excellence to Five Paradigm Shifts, it can be overwhelming to keep all of the concepts in mind. This chapter corresponds with Appendix B, a two-page blueprint summarizing the Five Paradigm Shifts in a customizable Action Plan to train flourishing. The term "dynamic" represents adjustments and changes you can make to the Action Plan as you grow and experience transitions in your life.

Blueprinting your Action Plan:

1. During Paradigm Shift 1 (Chapter 6), you explored questions that helped develop a relationship with your values. Utilizing that values relationship, in Paradigm Shift 2 (Chapter 7) you listed what healthy and unhealthy expressions of your values look like in action. Now transfer the values and descriptions that feel most relevant from that list to your Action Plan in Appendix B.
2. Paradigm Shift 3 (Chapter 8) looked at six strategies for managing fear differently. In the "Personalizing the concepts" section, we asked you to pick one strategy that you'd like to be more mindful of. Transfer that fear management strategy to the indicated section of your Action Plan.
3. Paradigm Shift 4 (Chapter 9) examined coping and self-care strategies. In the "Personalizing the concepts" section, you were asked to choose one Effective Coping Step that feels most relevant to you at this time in your life. You also chose one self-care practice that works for you and one that you'd like to try. Transfer these choices to the indicated section of your Action Plan along with any training that may be involved.
4. At the bottom of the second page in Appendix B you'll see the five daily action steps discussed in Paradigm Shift 5 (Chapter 10) for developing an expressive mindset.

This is your personal mental training program. In the same way that you wouldn't expect to do well on a test you didn't study for, you can't expect to consistently flourish without working at it. Fear-based responses are so natural and practiced that it takes training to move beyond those neurological patterns. This Action Plan is a powerful form of that training. On two pages, you have your current personal truth and what that specifically looks like in action. You have your most relevant fear management strategy, your most relevant coping strategy, and five steps to help you approach your day with expression rather than fear. Take a picture of your Action Plan and be mindful of its components every day.

Moving from fear-based neurological patterns to a place of Authentic Excellence never becomes totally automatic. The Fear-Based Model of Excellence is too entrenched in our thinking, behavior, and society.

Flourishing may not become involuntary, but this work does become less burdensome and greatly increases our resilience, productivity, and fulfillment. Even when we develop a rhythm with this material, something can happen in our lives that will interrupt our progression. Our world does not foster authentic excellence, so it requires intentionality and practice to put us in a more flourishing, resilient place. It is important to be aware of how life can pull us away from flourishing and to accept the work it takes to move beyond our neurology: "I will accept this work and practice for the benefit of my flourishing." Your individual flourishing and health changes our world.

Key point

1. It takes training to move beyond fear-based neurological responses. The Action Plan (Appendix B) distills the Five Paradigm Shifts into a personalized training program for flourishing.

Notes

Part III

Special considerations for flourishing and resilience

12 Values profile of young adults

If you had told Marlena five years ago that she'd be living in her hometown working for her family's car dealership, she would have laughed at you. However, there were benefits in working for the family business. At the age of 22, she had saved up five grand, paid her own bills, and had enough to money in her checking account to live far more comfortably than most of her friends from high school. "You're a Manager," her friend envied. "You have a real job. I'm broke and have no idea what I'm going to do after art school."

"Keep painting. I don't even remember the last time I did any art."

"Yeah, but I'm never going to make any money. My dad would've paid for a 'normal' college, but I had to go to art school. You don't have to worry about money."

Marlena thought about what her uncle had said to her that morning. "You should've saved up enough money for a down payment on a house by now. You gotta be smart with your money. You'd be crazy not to get a whole-life insurance policy at your age."

Marlena felt unhealthy. She hadn't been able to work out or go hiking in weeks. The hours spent proving that she could sell and manage the business's books, plus the hours spent networking with customers and winning over staff with dinners, bar tabs, and community outings, had worn her down.

"What I wouldn't give to go hiking in the park and sketch some landscapes," Marlena pictured. "There's gotta be a better way to deal with paying your dues."

Now that you've studied the Fear-Based Model of Excellence in Part I and gone through the Authentic Excellence training program in Part II, in Part III we will address issues that can have a particular impact on flourishing and resilience. The following chapters will explore how the values of young adults, transition, stress, sensitivity, giftedness, creativity, leadership, team development, and decision-making can heighten our vulnerability to the plateau effect.

In 2018, we analyzed Life Values Inventory data from 117,449 young adults aged 17–29 to explore common values. Below is a summary of the results.

Values profile of emerging and young adults, aged 17–29, *n* = 117,449

High Priority

"These values are important to me and I frequently act on them."

> Values: Responsibility
> Achievement
> Concern for Others
> Independence

Over-Attention

"I am devoting <u>more</u> attention to these values than I would prefer."

> Values: Belonging
> Financial Prosperity
> Interdependence

Under-Attention

"I am devoting <u>less</u> attention to these values than I would prefer."

> Values: Concern for the Environment
> Health and Activity
> Creativity
> Spirituality

Medium/Low Priority

"These values are less important and I don't act on them very frequently."

> Values: Concern for the Environment
> Spirituality
> Privacy
> Objective Analysis
> Humility

As you may remember, High Priority values are the values we find important and frequently act on. There is a sense of integrity associated with these values because they are aligned with our behavior. However, High Priority values can lead us to expect equity. Since we are acting on these values frequently, we hope that we will get a return on our efforts. Look at the values that matter most to emerging and young adults. These values reflect that young adults today want to be dependable and trustworthy (Responsibility), they want to challenge themselves to grow and excel (Achievement), they want to develop a sense of autonomy and self-sufficiency (Independence), and they care about the wellbeing of others (Concern for Others). Such values can move cultural change toward flourishing. But flourishing only occurs if the vulnerabilities of these values are managed well. High Priority values can lead to stress because their level of importance involves higher stakes. Many young adults find these values to be important, act on them, and expect that their actions will lead to good outcomes. What if those positive outcomes do not occur? What if young adults do their part but other factors prevent them from attaining fair and equitable results? That uncertainty accounts for a lot of the stress that young adults describe feeling today. And many manage that uncertainty through anxious over-control or guilt-ridden avoidance. At their healthiest, young adults are embracing these values and defining their success by their efforts toward such a purpose. At their unhealthiest, young adults are chronically evaluating themselves based on the equity or fairness of the outcomes they receive for their efforts.

Over-Attention values have worry and insecurity attached to them. Worry can cause us to over-focus on these values, making them feel like "have to"s rather than values of meaning. The summary profile of young adults demonstrates a sense of worry and less security about Belonging (feeling included and accepted in work and social groups), Financial Prosperity (experiencing financial success), and Interdependence (respecting traditions and making decisions based on one's connection within a family or group). It makes sense that so many young adults are devoting more attention than they would prefer to these values. At this stage in life young adults are often redefining themselves among new groups of peers and feel the "need" to be accepted and included. Young adults are also establishing careers and becoming self-sufficient as financial providers. Also, at this time in their lives many young adults are readjusting their place within their family structure. All of these factors imbue these values with over-attention, insecurity, and worry. If these values are not managed well, they can become sources of chronic anxiety that are either characterized by intensity and over-control, or by avoidance through safer forms of relating (e.g., social media).

If we're over-attending to some values, it means that by necessity we are under-attending to other values. It's interesting to note that the data indicates that young adults' over-attention to Belonging, Financial Prosperity, and Interdependence comes at the cost of values that are related to wellness: Concern for the Environment, Health and Activity, Creativity, and Spirituality. This cost has implications for sustainability and resilience. If the stress of our High Priority and Over-Attention values causes us to lose touch with our own sense of wellness, our connection to the environment, our connection to something larger than ourselves, or expanding our mind creatively, that cost can decrease our ability to sustain a consistent level of productivity, resilience, and fulfillment. Remember, we have little time and energy left after attending to our High Priority and Over-Attention values. So, it can help to focus on just one Under-Attention value rather than set an expectation to focus on all of your Under-Attention values.

For young adults, Concern for the Environment and Spirituality were split between Under-Attention and Medium/Low Priority relative to High Priority values. Many young adults found Privacy, Objective Analysis, and Humility to be Medium/Low Priority values in relation to other values at this stage in their lives. It can help to be aware of this data if these values are High Priority or Over-Attention values for you. For instance, if you are a young adult who values Privacy as a High Priority value, your peers may not understand the importance and health of your actions that derive from the value of Privacy. Furthermore, there may be fewer opportunities to act on Privacy amidst a peer group that generally views that value as a Medium/Low Priority. Additionally, if you are not a young adult but regularly interact with young adults, it can help to have an understanding of this data. For instance, it can be easy to judge a young adult who does not exhibit humility in their behavior, especially if Humility is a High Priority or Over-Attended value for you. Rather than draw conclusions about a young person's behavior, it can be beneficial to objectively look at that behavior as the result of Humility being a Low Priority value just as you might view a value like Belonging as a Low Priority value.

Understanding data on group values can help us remain actively curious and open in our experiences with others. However, be mindful not to assign or judge individuals based on group trends. When we utilize values as a platform to understand and relate to ourselves and others, we can flourish on a more consistent basis.

Key points

1. Values data from 117,449 young adults aged 17–29 indicates that young adults today (2018) generally want to be dependable and trustworthy (Responsibility), they want to challenge themselves to grow and excel (Achievement), they want to develop a sense of autonomy and self-sufficiency (Independence), and they care about the wellbeing of others (Concern for Others).
2. The summary profile of young adults demonstrates a sense of worry and less security about Belonging, Financial Prosperity, and Interdependence.
3. The data shows that young adults' over-attention to Belonging, Financial Prosperity, and Interdependence comes at the cost of values that are related to wellness: Health and Activity, Concern for the Environment, Spirituality, and Creativity. This cost has implications for sustainability and resilience.
4. Understanding how a group's general values compare with the relationship we have with our own values can help us interact with others in more efficient and fulfilling ways.

Personalizing the concepts

1. What were your first impressions of the group profile for young adults?
2. How does your individual values profile compare to the group profile for young adults? What factors create similarities or differences?

Notes

13 Sensitivity, giftedness, and values

The active-minded, active-hearted young adult

"You're my best friend."

"Umm, ok."

"Am I your best friend?"

"I dunno."

Russell came home to find his son crying again. "RJ, you're being way too sensitive… You've gotta stop harping on things like this." Russell was becoming increasingly concerned about his son's development. How was RJ going to survive his teenage years if he continued to be so intense and unable to let things go?

As an adult RJ began dating Sylvia. She was a state assembly staffer working hard to climb the ranks. RJ was a talented chef who could anticipate dining trends like a psychic and restaurateurs were beginning to take notice. Sylvia made the effort to accommodate their different lifestyles; yes, he drank more than she did, yes, he was a bit OCD, but he saw things in her and in life that were rare for a person to see.

On their second date RJ showed up and gave her a toy watch. "What's this?"

"It's your retirement watch… You work so hard to get ahead. So, congratulations, you're ahead… achieved, retired. You won't feel pressure at work anymore."

"Haha, because I'm retired?"

"Exactly."

She kept the toy watch on her desk because the joke helped calm her during tough moments at work. Sylvia had dated people in the past who hadn't understood her drive and stress like RJ had in one date. However, despite the great start to their relationship, the past two weeks had been rocky.

The trouble started when they had run into her ex-boyfriend. RJ had peripherally known Sylvia's ex through work which expounded his jealousy. Two weeks later, RJ was still struggling to let go of his intense feelings surrounding the ex. Sylvia could see the internal struggle within RJ. On the one hand, he knew that her past had nothing to do with him, but on the other hand, he couldn't prevent himself from being consumed by his emotions. It eventually deteriorated the relationship.

Six years later, RJ knew he had to make a change. He was lonely, drinking too much, driving his staff crazy, and despite opening three successful restaurants, investors had stopped calling. His therapist had repeatedly pointed out that it was a gift to be sensitive and analytical if he could manage the challenges in a healthy way. It was time to find new ways to manage himself before his life got too far off track.

He committed to four steps. The first was exercising three times a week. The second was giving up control of one of his restaurants. He had a fully capable and trustworthy employee who should've been promoted to General Manager ages ago. The third step was practicing Natural Vagus Nerve Stimulation using diaphragmatic breathing. Every day for five minutes he would clear his mind, breathe into his diaphragm for four seconds, hold his breath for four seconds, and breathe out through pursed lips for four seconds. The fourth step he committed to was taking a minute every day to find an example of his sensitivity and analytical nature that he appreciated. "Everyone said my restaurants would fail if I insisted on paying my staff as much as I do, and those are the same owners who drop hundreds of thousands on décor, underpay their staff, and wonder why they're scraping by. I wouldn't have gone against those doubts if I wasn't sensitive and analytical."

After a couple months of committing to his four steps, RJ noticed a natural inclination to expand upon his shift in behavior. He even considered giving Sylvia Banes a call after he saw a newspaper article depicting the new city council woman at her desk with a toy watch in the background.

Much attention has been paid in recent years to understanding the power and gift of sensitivity and vulnerability (Aron, 1997; Brown, 2012; Neff, 2011). Sensitivity can lead to remarkable insights and expressions, and it can also amplify the pressures and fears of life to overwhelming levels. Values work can be instrumental in helping young adults who are sensitive harness the power of sensitivity rather than trying to suppress it.

Many people distinguish emotional sensitivity and objective analysis as separate perspectives that do not cohabitate. Individuals may be emotionally sensitive and not very analytical, or highly analytical and not very emotionally sensitive. But there are some individuals who are both. They are emotionally sensitive and highly analytical. We refer to them as active-minded, active-hearted individuals. People who are emotionally sensitive but not very analytical are primarily guided by their feelings and can find resolution with a change in their emotions. People who are analytical and not very emotionally sensitive are primarily guided by their thoughts and can function within the world through their logic and analysis. Active-minded, active-hearted (AM/AH) individuals are emotionally attuned to themselves and their surroundings, and when they are moved emotionally, they think deeply about their experience. These individuals can have trouble dismissing challenging experiences until their feelings and thoughts are resolved. Their range of emotional faculty allows them to experience profound beauty and joy in life, but it can also contribute to experiences of profound pain.

Oftentimes AM/AH individuals are aware of their heightened sensitivity at a very young age. As children, they feel acutely aware of details, and pick up on emotions around them before others seem to. And because they are children, they are often overwhelmed by their sensitivity. They may also receive feedback from others that they are "too sensitive", or are made to feel like their sensitivity is a weakness. Based on those experiences, sensitive children may seek to suppress their sensitivity through over-control or avoidance, and entrench the Fear-Based Model of Excellence into their pattern of living. As young adults, this pattern for managing the intensity of living an emotionally analytical life will start to work against them. Suppressing one's authentic gift of sensitivity through over-control and avoidance is not sustainable. Fear-Based Model of Excellence coping strategies such as over-control and avoidance can inhibit the benefits of being AM/AH while leading to increasing physical and mental strain.

An avoidant coping pattern AM/AH individuals may fall into is excessive substance use. The intensity of being sensitive and analytical begs for relief. The most instant forms of relief are food, drugs, sex, pain/exercise, and compelling entertainment (e.g., movies, TV, gaming, shopping). So it is natural to seek these out for reprieve because they can quickly alter the brain chemistry. While substances can provide temporary avoidance-comfort, they can also be deceptive. Frequent and/or high quantity usage of substances can actually magnify and distort the already-intense emotions and deep thoughts one is trying to avoid. Self-care and self-compassion are important countermeasures because punishing oneself over substance use can lead to more substance use. Over time, the relief and ability to achieve outcomes through substance-avoidance can eventually deteriorate.

AM/AH individuals can also exhibit controlling and perfectionistic behaviors to deal with the pressures of being emotionally sensitive and analytical. Remember, AM/AH adults can struggle in dismissing and moving on from situations until their feelings and thoughts are resolved. This can lead to strain when aspects of an experience that are beyond one's control prevent resolution. Crippling worry and over-thought are common inhibitors for AM/AH individuals, which can at times develop into OCD behaviors as a form of relief when their thoughts or feelings can't be resolved. The uncertainty surrounding experiences AM/AH individuals find important, such as a performance or a relationship, can cause that individual to try and control elements of the experience to involve feelings and thoughts that they are more comfortable dealing with intensely.

Avoidance and over-control patterns of coping can sometimes turn into attributes AM/AH individuals identify with. This identification can mislead one to thinking that part of what makes them unique is their suffering, avoidance, or perfectionism. Identity misconceptions can be reinforced when a community builds around such identities. The fear-based coping patterns of dealing with AM/AH challenges can be seen as what is unique about a person, rather than the beauty and power of being sensitive and analytical. Not only does suppressing sensitivity and analysis take an unsustainable mental and physical toll, but it also prevents one from experiencing the benefits of being sensitive and analytical. AM/AH individuals can be power-fully empathetic to the world and to others. They can see opportunities for expression through avenues that may not be visible to most people. They can develop insights and communicate original ideas that strongly resonate with others. When AM/AH individuals appreciate the benefits of their sensitivity and analysis instead of suppressing them, they can experience powerful flourishing. The goal is to honor and embrace this expanded range of emotional and cognitive ability while managing the amplified pain and intensity in a healthy manner.

Giftedness

Let's revisit RJ from the example above when he was a child.

While his parents were concerned about RJ's sensitivity, they were reassured to see him gravitate toward a particular interest. "RJ, put that knife down!" his mother yelled the first time she found him trying to mimic the way Julia Child was cutting an onion on TV. His parents started encouraging RJ's experimentation in the kitchen and were stunned when he began to cook meals that had a precision and originality beyond what most adults could accomplish. "RJ you're so talented."

RJ's parents began to host dinner parties to show off their son's talent. "I'm so impressed." "Your son has such a gift." "This is incredible." "He's only 11 years old?" These accolades fed RJ who was craving some kind of substantiation in his young life.

As he entered his teenage years, his reputation as a gifted chef started to become a burden. He questioned himself in the kitchen rather than enjoying the experimentation. "Would adding rosemary impress them or just taste weird?"

RJ began to distance himself from culinary pursuits as the pressure to live up to expectations mounted and high school bullies began to make fun of his talent. He would not rediscover an interest in cooking until his mid-twenties.

It can be difficult to manage the expectations and pressures associated with possessing a gift that our society deems extraordinary. When children or emerging adults exhibit talent, they can be labeled as gifted, special, or talented. These labels can amplify all the elements of the Fear-Based Model of Excellence. As emerging adults grow with their talent, a need can develop to live up to the label of "gifted". Because the gifted label often gets attached to someone at a young age, they are vulnerable to identity foreclosure (Chickering & Reisser, 1993; Crace, 2008) where they completely define their self-worth by their gift. The concept of unrealized potential can intensify fear of failure and chronic evaluation which leads to natural coping patterns like over-control and avoidance. Young adults can experience the shame and judgment of not living up to their label. They can also exhaust themselves with worry and over-preparation.

The label of "gifted" or "talented" may not be the only reason fear can be overwhelming. Emerging adults may also have an intrinsic love for the medium of their talent. As we have learned, fear has a dynamic relationship with values. If something is important to us, there are stakes involved. Whether it be a label, an intrinsic interest, or both, emerging adults can over-identify their self-worth with their talent. This identification can greatly increase pressure and fear.

It can help AM/AH and "gifted" young adults to develop a supportive sense of appreciation and respect for their sensitivity, analysis, and gifts. Being sensitive and analytical is a gift. The combination of an active mind and an active heart allows individuals to connect their deep feelings and thoughts to values that provide meaning and purpose. Paradigm Shifts 1 (Chapter 6) and 2 (Chapter 7) help train awareness of healthy and unhealthy expressions of our gifts and talents. Paradigm Shifts 4 (Chapter 9) and 5 (Chapter 10) help develop routines of self-care, coping strategies, and daily values-based thinking that puts fear and emotions in their optimal place for flourishing. The work is about clarifying a personal truth and holding that meaning in a healthy manner, even when expressing a talent or thinking and feeling deeply.

Key points

1. Active-minded, active-hearted (AM/AH) individuals are emotionally attuned to themselves and their surroundings, and when they are moved emotionally, they think deeply about their experience.
2. The intensity of being acutely sensitive and analytical begs for relief. Managing the gift of sensitivity through over-control and avoidance is not sustainable.
3. Emerging adults can feel pressure to live up to labels like "gifted" or "talented". They are also vulnerable to over-identifying their self-worth with these labels.
4. Developing routines of self-care, coping strategies, and daily values-based thinking can help people embrace the fight to flourish as an AM/AH individual.

Personalizing the concepts

1. What is your relationship to emotional sensitivity and objective analysis?
2. How do you manage the challenges of being sensitive, analytical, or both? What is a coping strategy you utilize that is not sustainable? What is a healthier coping strategy you can practice (see Chapter 9 for coping strategies and self-care)?
3. Is there someone close to you that is AM/AH? How do you manage their challenges and attributes in your interactions?

References

Aron, E. (1997). *The highly sensitive person.* New York: Broadway Books.

Brown, B. (2012). *Daring greatly: How the courage to be vulnerable transforms the way we live, love, parent, and lead.* New York: Gotham.

Chickering, A.W., & Reisser, L. (1993). *Education and identity.* San Francisco, CA: Jossey-Bass.

Crace, R.K. (2008, January). *Optimal self-leadership principles for parents of high ability students.* Workshop presented at the annual meeting of the Center for Gifted Education Conference, Williamsburg, VA.

Neff, K. (2011). *Self-compassion: The proven power of being kind to yourself.* New York: HarperCollins.

Notes

14 Creativity and values

Luke's dad didn't share any of his secret hopes when he brought home the piano. Maybe one of his kids would take to it, maybe not. When Luke, who barely had all his baby teeth, started climbing up on the bench to concoct valid tonal motifs, the family was blown away. Even Luke's mom, who was concerned about her husband's level of enthusiasm, permitted an intense level of attention to cultivate young Luke's talent.

There were music lessons, teachers, recitals, travel, summer camps, performing arts schools, pressure. So much pressure.

The unraveling was only noticeable to Luke and a couple of teachers during his teenage years. However, his talent carried him to a renowned conservatory.

At the conservatory things began to come apart. He was no longer a big fish in a small pond. He was a small fish in an ocean. Students at the conservatory were scary, not because they were proficient, but because many of them seemed to enjoy playing. There was a natural ease in their approach. They weren't forcing anything. They were creating sound in a place beyond method or technique. For the first time, Luke saw a limit to his career as a musician.

At first, he denied the limitation; maybe if he just worked harder he'd get to that next level. He thought he was one book away, one class away, one concept away from unlocking the secret. The expectations to live up to his giftedness grew louder as a wall began to develop. Physical atrophy and apathy toward the instrument set in.

Luke limped toward a degree and then moved to New York. He lied to his parents about recording and playing regular gigs. In actuality, Luke was living for the first time. He got a bartending job, made real friends, and enjoyed being free from music.

Luke didn't miss playing music, but he missed performing. One night a friend coerced him on stage for a stand-up comedy open mic. Luke did a few minutes and actually got some laughs. He was hooked.

Six years later, Luke was performing three to four times a week. Building material was difficult, but he was learning to find his voice. His delivery and stage presence was at an all-time high. He had a large social media following. Agents and bookers were remembering his name.

He loved comedy, but it was a slog. He was 32 and felt the fatigue of the service industry. What else could he do to make money and still do comedy?

There was no way his heartbroken parents could understand his accolades or frustrations. By now they had forgone the pain of Luke not being Mozart and were just trying to "save their lost son". They offered deals: "Why don't you open a business? Draft a business plan and we might invest?" Or, "We'll loan you the money to go back to school and get your MBA. With your ability to talk to people you could be a successful businessman."

The frustrations of artistic life made the offers tempting. Luke was struggling to deal with difficult customers at his job, bombing a set here and there, watching younger comics getting big breaks. He felt like quitting, except… he knew that he had no choice. Luke would always want to do stand-up no matter how that affected other aspects of his life. "So how am I gonna live out the rest of my days as a comedian?"

LVI for the creative life

Creativity is an important value that drives many people to devote their lives to creative projects and artistic performances. This chapter reexamines Paradigm Shift 1, moving from values clarification to values relationship, in the context of an artist. It can be difficult to manage the expectations, pressures, and consequent coping patterns associated with being creative, but managing these challenges is the burden of the artist not the art. Art and expression are abstract practices that are tied to a creative energy. The more an artist can move beyond their neurological responses to the human pressure of the creative world, the more likely the artist will be to flourish and flow with artistic expression. In this chapter, we will delve deeper into subcategories of the Creativity value and examine creative life roles. In doing so, we will look at concepts that can help the creative mind find meaningful expression and resilience.

We will subdivide the Creativity value into five Creative Expressions:

1. Creation and Project Construction
2. Learning Technique
3. Brainstorming and Outlining
4. Performing
5. Editing and Organizing

Just as we've customized the value of Creativity into subcategories, it can be helpful to expound one's life roles to more accurately fit a creative lifestyle. The LVI provides three common life roles: Work/Academic, Relationships, Leisure and Community Activities. The Work/Academics role can be further divided into creative subcategories to give six life roles:

1. Income Work
2. Art Career
3. Other Mediums
4. Art Adjacent Work

5. Relationships
6. Leisure and Community Activities

Creative Expressions

Creation and Project Construction

Creation and Project Construction involves manifesting imagination into a realized work or performance. This creative value entails creating a work that acts as a conduit between one's mind and another's. Manifesting a representation of one's imagination can be frustrating and call on natural responses to fear such as perfectionism and avoidance. Although important, it is never easy to come from an expressive mindset rather than an outcome-oriented mindset when building creative projects. Focusing on the outcome of finishing a project can work against you by pulling you away from imagination and expression. It can be helpful to view building work only as an opportunity to express your art.

There is a misconception that because one greatly values creating art one will have a fulfilling experience in the real-time creating and constructing of works. Dorothy Parker said, "I hate writing but love having written." The more we care about the work the more stakes are involved, which can create pressure when combined with uncertainty associated with the ambiguous nature of art. Leading with expression and our values instead of fear can help keep this pressure in the background. When we lead with expression, we put ourselves in a better position to work with the art. Many times artistic works develop a life or momentum of their own. If we are preoccupied with fear, pressure, or evaluation, it is harder to flow with the natural progression art often provides us.

It is important to be aware of how the challenges of this Creative Expression can greatly affect other aspects of an individual's life. When frustrated with the expression of the Creation and Project Construction, one's mood, health, and relating abilities can be impacted, amplifying challenges in other life roles. Although Creation and Project Construction might not be as immediately fulfilling as Performing, for example, focusing on the opportunity to freely express your creativity can allow you to draw upon a deeper source of motivation.

Artists can often become chronically evaluative of the amount or perceived quality of their completed works as an indication of their worth as an artist. You are an artist and you are enough regardless of how much or how little you express Creation and Project Construction. When we don't feel "enough" as artists, we can start to rely heavily on outcomes and completed works to reassure our worth. Focusing on outcomes can commodify creative works into forms that have little to do with imagination and art.

As in yoga, think of artistic expression as a form of practice. Sometimes we can be so worn down by trying to realize an imagined idea that all we may be able to muster is a going-through-the-motions minimal practice. This is a successful practice of creative expression. Defining success by expression can connect us with imagination and play, which can allow the life of a work to better interact with our imagination, resulting in more flourishing expressions.

Learning Technique

Learning Technique is a major component of artistic development. There are many ways to study and internalize techniques, such as through specialized schools, published works, self-discovery, and mentorship. It is a Creative Expression that can ebb and flow throughout an artist's life. Learning Technique can be heavily attended to at the beginning of an artist's development where pure imagination couples with an individual's gravitation to a medium. One learns technique by repeating methods used by others and experimentation. Over time, experience begins to accumulate to the point where artists are able to communicate the language of a medium through their own interpretation of technique.

Many artists find fulfillment expressing Learning Technique by teaching. Artists who teach can utilize this expression in the creative life roles of Income Work, Art Adjacent Work, or even as the main focus of their Art Career. There are many creative minds that after years of focusing on their own work find fulfillment in teaching others technique based on their experiences.

Artists are sometimes vulnerable to devote too much energy toward Learning Technique as a form of never-ending preparation, which can be a way of avoiding important but scary expressions like Performing and Creation and Project Construction. In creativity, moving too far away from imagination and play can result in burnout. Let's revisit Luke's example at the beginning of the chapter.

As the instrument began to slip away from Luke, there would be the occasional spark of interest. He'd connect with a song and say to himself, "I should go home and just play that song for fun." He'd go home to play, but would try to transcribe the song by ear. If he struggled to transcribe the song, he would get scared that his abilities were weakening and either force himself to transcribe or abandon the song in frustration. Luke wouldn't allow himself to look up sheet music just to have some quick fun playing a song, which was exactly what his music life needed.

Brainstorming and Outlining

Brainstorming and Outlining involves the formulation of ideas, a courtship to the eventual marriage of abstract imagination and manifested work. This Creative Expression is less a foundation for Creation and Project Construction and more a crystallization of pure imagination. This value is rooted in "play". There is an improvisation in forming and spit-balling ideas.

Brainstorming and Outlining can allow someone to express their imagination without judgment or edits. Technique can be applied as little or as much as the artist desires. It's noodling around on the guitar; improvising comedy in conversation; languaging poems, lyrics, and prose; it's sketching out a design; splashing paint on a wall; blocking the outline of a story idea.

Many artists experience fulfillment by stockpiling ideas that may never get touched. Brainstorming and Outlining may be an artist's primary relationship with creativity. Some artists rarely take their art beyond the Brainstorming and Outlining expression. This focus does not discount one's substance as an artist even if that individual doesn't identify as an artist. Some of the best creative partners and editing minds one can work with are "ideas people".

Performing

Performing is a Creative Expression that asks a lot of an artist. There are constant challenges performers face: hitting certain technical marks, staying in a present mindset, managing audience reaction, etc. Despite the challenges, one can experience powerful fulfillment when performing. Performing is the attempt to become fully in the present moment of pure expression while an audience participates in the experience. This is extremely challenging in a world driven by outcomes.

As discussed in Chapter 7, our performances can benefit by understanding what a healthy expression of Performing looks like in action and when that expression begins to exhibit unhealthy characteristics. For example, "A healthy expression of Performing is when I'm coming from a place of imagination, play, and presence. When that crosses the line into being evaluative, 'Does that look right? Does the director think I'm a good actor? This doesn't sound good. Does the audience like me?' I'm Performing in an unhealthy way." Having an idea of this boundary can help center an artist in real time when unhealthy components begin to inhibit performance.

Another effective source to utilize when performing is volitional confidence (discussed in Chapter 8). "When I feel that I can't, what of this *can* I do?" Volitional confidence can help focus one's energy on a manageable portion where one can better connect to imagination and expression. This practice can guide you to perform better when you don't have your "A" game. Despite those rare times when everything falls into place, there are many incredible performances that don't begin well but blossom into magic. It is rare to start off with your "A" game and maintain it. Many great performances start off as a "B" performance in terms of flow and rise to an "A+" by the performer staying calm during adversity, accepting challenges, and trusting themself.

Regarding audience awareness, there is a fine line between unhealthy evaluation and healthy analysis. Using the audience to inform the direction and development of a performance is perfectly fine because it's more of an objective creative analysis. For example, choosing to go big with a character to give the audience a larger sense of departure is a creative decision. However, it can inhibit expression to view an audience reaction as a personal statement of your creativity: "I'm a bad actor" or "I'm a great musician." Positive audience reactions can also be misleading. It feels great to receive positive audience feedback, but if one takes it as a personal statement, "I'm a great musician; I know what I'm doing," it can cause one to be too reliant on an audience's reaction. Any audience reaction is subjective. Negative and positive reactions can be misinformed and inaccurate. When analysis of an audience crosses into personal evaluation of oneself, it can work against the artist's expression and development.

Audience response and outcomes only have as much to do with artistic expression as you let them. Artistic expression can be viewed as practice. Let your art be enough and trust your innate ability to be enough just by practicing. Defining success as the expression of Creativity can help anchor one in a deeper place of motivation, resilience, and flow. Sometimes in a performance the stars simply do not align and sometimes they do regardless of any reason, understanding, or intention. The unknown nature of art can be scary when it is so important to us. One can help manage these challenges by focusing on imagination, expression, and practice.

Editing and Organizing

The Editing and Organizing Creative Expression can be one of the more trying expressions an artist manages. It is difficult to bring a work of creativity to a place of "done-ness". Some creative minds find this expression to be their preferred relationship to Creativity. Other creative people can avoid or be perfectionistic when expressing Editing and Organizing. When we devote more attention to a value (or Creative Expression) than we prefer, we can experience stress. Many times, when a project progresses to the point where editing and organizing is needed, the artist may already be exhausted and vulnerable. When experiencing such unrest, stress, or burnout, it is important to trust the temporary nature of this over-attention for a greater rightness. A project that is an important manifestation of your creativity is asking for a challenging amount of attention and expression to reach a form of realized art.

Editing can be very uncomfortable, especially when dealing with a project that has already required so much risk and effort. It is difficult to revisit the difficulties and depths one took repeatedly for the sake of technical refinement. It is important to realize the difficulty of this challenge and exercise healthy coping and self-care strategies (discussed in Chapter 9).

Another challenging component of expressing Editing and Organizing is the ambiguous nature of "done-ness". Many times it is not clear as to when an artist transitions from creating to editing, and there is certainly no definitive end to the editing and organizing of a project. The argument that there are no completed works of art has merit because one can endlessly edit and organize. Author David Mitchell says he knows he's done editing when he starts changing items back to their original state. Mitchell's idea is one guideline, but the editing process is different for each artist and varies from project to project. An artist develops an instinctual gauge with certain projects and their overall editing process.

There are a number of artists that find Editing and Organizing to be a fulfilling expression of art at certain times in their artistic life. Elevating and contributing to others' works in progress can be a meaningful form of art. Artists can practice this Creative Expression through life roles such as Income Work, Art Adjacent Work, and Art Career.

The inherent nature of editing can be a deflating experience. Transitioning an inspiring idea into a concrete form can feel like failure. Cutting and shaping aspects of an artistic expression can be difficult, painful, and confusing. Trust that the magic of the work is not lost in the technicalities of editing. The power of the work is shifting from the artist's imagination to the audience's creative participation. The work is becoming its true form, a conduit of imagination. It can help to trust the reader or audience. A work of art is a communal effort. The reader/audience is participating in the work. It can be easy to lose sight of this when editing your creative idea into a digestible format. Insecurity can cause an artist to overstress a point or, as acclaimed writer Ted Thompson explains, "bully the reader." It can help to trust the reader or audience to meet your expression however their imagination chooses to dance with your work.

Creative life roles

Income Work

Income Work is a life role that can be a major source of stress in a creative person's life. Some find Financial Prosperity to be not an important value beyond the point of facilitating their artistic pursuits. Other creatives may view Financial Prosperity as an important value that conflicts with Creativity. Either way, a person has to negotiate money in order to pay bills. Many times artists acquire money by spending time and energy in fields they may not like. It can help to draw a distinction between one's creative life roles and Income Work. An artist is often called to spend a substantial amount of time and energy on Income Work. Some artists live as inexpensively as possible and sacrifice creature comforts, some artists work part-time jobs to maximize time to devote to creative work, other artists work financially stable jobs and sacrifice preferred time to work on their creative projects, and many fluctuate between these options.

Challenges can arise when an artist experiences rewarding outcomes and approval in their Income Work. These outcomes can feel satisfying especially when we are receiving few desired outcomes in our creative life. Income Work outcomes can prompt one to agree to more Income Work responsibilities which will require more time and energy. It is important to be aware of the significance creative expression can have on your wellness when prioritizing large decisions.

It can be defeating to spend consistent time and energy on Income Work we don't like. Stress and frustration are natural responses, but if they become too much of the focus it can center us in a place of resentment. It can help to focus on underlying purposes: "I'm spending time on this work to pay bills in order to have space to create my art." This focus can root artists in a deeper source of resilience because it's tied to the value of Creativity.

Art Career

This creative life role embodies one's artistic life. It involves artistic development, creative output, and desired focus of an artist's energies. It may help to view this life role as one's current primary medium. If you had all the money in the world, where and how would you devote your creative energies in a fulfilling way? If you had no money, how would you express your creative energies? Time and energy management can benefit by distinguishing the Art Career life role as the platform in which you express your most important creative energies.

Other Mediums

Ron was primarily an actor until his mid-twenties. He had gained experience in performance and technique through this medium, but had also become so outcome-oriented that debilitating pressure began to overwhelm him. The ability and desire to bridge the gap between acting technique and expression became less important to Ron. As a result, acting was no longer fulfilling his creative value, so Ron naturally gravitated to writing as an outlet. It started out as an exercise to influence his acting, but because he was able to connect to expression and imagination more easily in this medium, Ron grew to focus on the medium of literature. Ten years later, Ron had relegated acting to the occasional hobby and had become a serious writer.

Artists can experience benefits by learning, observing, and participating in mediums other than their primary focus. There is a wealth of concepts and methods that when crossed over to a new medium align to create fulfilling art, and conversely add rich new perspectives to mediums of primary focus. Some artists are very serious about several mediums and other artists concentrate on one. Using other mediums can help an artist reconnect to one's core imagination because a different medium challenges the artist to rely more on pure artistic expression rather than on experienced proficiency. All mediums influence each other. Artists can draw from the benefits of other mediums by experiencing them as an audience member.

Creative expression through different mediums does not prevent the difficulties and discomfort that inherently come with expressing art. However, sometimes different mediums click more succinctly with one's expression at different times in a creative person's life.

Art Adjacent Work

This creative life role involves work that is closely related to one's Art Career, but more rooted in career development, exposure, networking, and money. Poets may find work as copywriters, actors may be called away from fulfilling roles for commercial work, painters may do graphic design work for advertising, etc.

This creative life role provides opportunities for creative expression but may not result in much fulfillment. Art Adjacent Work can involve self-promotion and networking which is often unfulfilling work for an artist, but necessary for Art Career development. The underlying purpose of devoting energy to this role is to provide more opportunities to express art.

There are a number of artists who may experience a fair amount of crossover between the life role of Income Work and the life role of Art Adjacent Work. If one makes a living from Art Adjacent Work, it can be helpful to realize that combination of these life roles. Conversely, artists can better express their energies by distinguishing Income Work, Art Adjacent Work, and Art Career as separate platforms.

Relationships

This life role coincides with the LVI model because it is a role that can be influential in an artist's life as well as provide opportunities for creative expression and satisfaction. Manifesting imagination is difficult or perhaps impossible to fully realize, but the artist is still inspired and finds meaning to conjure physical representations of the inner imagination. Similarly, the idea of a relationship may never be fully realized because we can never be fully outside of our own experience; however, we are often inspired and find meaning in relating and experiencing love.

It is important to keep in mind that after energies are expended on life roles like Income Work and Art Career, one is left with little energy to relate to others. However, relating and spending time with friends and loved ones can still be an important value one finds fulfillment in expressing. Values prioritization in the context of a specific day's "rightness" is necessary for accommodating the importance one may feel in relating to others. When energy is low, remember to focus on relating (not the state of the relationship), self-care, and active curiosity.

Leisure and Community Activities

This life role also corresponds with the LVI model because Leisure and Community Activities can provide important opportunities for values fulfillment. This role involves activities that you choose to do with your personal time. They might include hobbies, social events, entertainment, exercise, volunteering, spiritual activities, or just spending quiet time alone.

People can misinterpret any time or energy spent outside of Income Work as leisure time. In the case of an artist, Art Career, Art Adjacent Work, and Income Work all require energy and present challenges that can be quite taxing. The benefit of designating Leisure and Community Activities outside creativity is to provide a clearer awareness of restoration and rest.

When artists juggle many life roles to facilitate their art, it is common to dismiss leisure time or become resentful about not experiencing sufficient restoration. Rest can be a vital tool for perspective, self-care, and imagination. There are periods of time when circumstances require specific life roles outside of art such as Income Work and Relationships to take priority over other life roles. During these periods, an artist may feel compelled to spend sparing moments on their art; however, the body, mind, and soul may also need rest during these spare moments. Rest and restoration can be centering acts of wellness that can benefit many aspects of one's life, including art.

One does not cease to be creative when one is not creating a project or performing. Taking time to rest, explore hobbies, participate in spontaneous events, and engage in the many Leisure and Community Activities outside of art can all help an artist tap into imagination, manifest art, and manage the challenges of a creative life.

Key points

1. There are several ways in which we express creativity. Distinguishing Creative Expressions that are important to us can help us better prioritize our values in the context of a day and allow us to tap into deeper sources of motivation and resilience.
2. Focusing on expression rather than evaluation is the most efficient portal to the imagination and increases the likelihood of flow experience.
3. Understanding the specialized definitions of creative life roles can foster effective values prioritization, and help one develop strategies to manage and cope with the challenges associated with non-creative life roles.

Personalizing the concepts

1. At this time in your life, what Creative Expression is most important to you? What is great about this expression, and what are the stresses and fears you have to manage when engaging in this expression?
2. What component in your life frequently inhibits Creativity? What is an underlying purpose or greater rightness associated with this inhibiting component? If there is no greater rightness or purpose, what are some steps you can take to change this conflicting element?
3. Define what imagination and play mean to you.

Notes

15 Transition and values

Kym sat down at her desk. She now had a desk... her own desk at a major newspaper. No more negotiating space with reckless roommates. No more glares from baristas as she indefinitely wrote in their small coffee shops. She was now an employed reporter. However, the more she scanned the notes for her first assignment, the more she felt like an imposter, "This angle doesn't work... does it? A lot of people are going to be reading this. I gotta re-interview everybody."

The owner of the bookstore began the staff meeting by introducing Rich, the new manager.

Rich was nervous. He felt like an imposter as he began a belabored speech about his direction for the store. An employee walked in 15 minutes late.

When the meeting concluded, Rich went up to the employee who had arrived late. "Hello, I'm Rich."

"Hi Rich, I'm John. Been here for five years—"

"John, I'm gonna need you to be here on time from now on."

"...Right, you see I'm in school and Brian said I didn't have to be here because—"

"Everybody else has lives, John, but they found a way to be here on time."

Kym had a strong web presence. Her articles and blogs had been read and shared by tens of thousands of readers. She had won awards at the university paper. Why was she doubting herself as an actual journalist? "Kym, you have to wrap up the transit piece by the end of the day or ditch it." Her editors were getting more and more stringent. She thought about quitting.

Rich spent the next month alienating his entire staff. It wasn't just the way he talked to them. It was his insistence on installing his own approach no matter how errant or ineffective the methodology was.

"He's clearly never worked in retail before," John complained to another staff member.

"I heard he worked in academia."

Rich interrupted the conversation, "Guys, I can't have you congregating on the floor... John, I thought you were going to switch the staff recommendations with the Young Adult section."

"Yes, but Rich, staff recommendations are our best sellers so we keep them by the entrance. We're kinda known for our picks and reviews."

"...I understand that, but we need to have more... more of a symmetrical look to the place and... Young Adult fiction sells."

"Kym, where is your voice? Where is the reporter we hired? This piece you turned in doesn't say anything."

"I was trying to cover all the angles."

"It's safe and... diluted—"

"I'm sorry."

"Don't say sorry. Snap out of it. We want you here. Do you want to be here?"

"Yes."

"Then be here."

It took three months for the owner to admit that the handful of staff departures, bad internet reviews, and concerning sales figures stemmed from his life-long buddy, Rich. Clearly the transition was not settling into a positive direction.

Transitions are stressful. Change is a necessary part of transition, and with change comes uncertainty. That high level of uncertainty around transitions naturally sparks components of the Fear-Based Model of Excellence. We can rely on outcomes to reassure us that we made the right decision. We can over-think and become more self-conscious as we work through the learning curve. In addition, transition usually means we will be letting go or losing something, which our mind processes as loss. It is natural to lead with fear instead of our values when managing the complicated challenges of transition.

Planned or proactive transitions

Planned transitions may include attending college, starting a first job, committing to an intimate relationship, having children, changing career, or retirement.

No matter how exciting or positive a planned transition may be, it can still be stressful and fearful due to the uncertainty. We are vulnerable to indecisiveness and inaction because we fear failure or making the wrong choices. We are also vulnerable to over-researching and over-planning elements of transition as an attempt to control the uncertainty surrounding change (Brown, 1995; Busacca, 2002; Busacca, Beebe, & Toman, 2010; Clemens & Milsom, 2008; Ercegovac & Koludrovic, 2012; Galassi, Crace, Martin, James, & Wallace, 1992; Galassi, Martin, Crace, & James, 1992).

Like Kym in the example above, we may have been successful in the past, but the uncertainties of the next transition cause us to doubt ourselves and our readiness for this next stage. We can struggle because we are so anxious and self-doubting that we either shut down or try to over-control everything around us. We need to have everything go smoothly at the beginning of the transition or we will use any difficulties as a sign that we are truly not ready or deserve this next stage.

Like Rich in the example above, we may assume that approaches we have used in the past will suffice in the next transition. We can be overconfident by rigidly incorporating the same model of success to new and different challenges. We can struggle because we are not attuned to information around us that will help us adapt our model of success to the new environment.

If we have relied on fear-based models of success, it is natural to apply that methodology to new stages in our lives. Responding to uncertainty, perceived evaluation, and cost through forms of over-control and avoidance has plateau effects, like endurance. Take the example of a college student transitioning into an intense career or graduate school environment. In college, a person can exhaust themselves for extended periods of time. "I just have to get to the end of the semester." There's an end point they reach where they can try to restore, but post-college, "pushing through" is unsustainable. We might be able to for a while, but eventually the Fear-Based Model of Excellence can start to detrimentally work against us. The world pushes us to break, but values can help us tap into the deeper sources of motivation and resilience. We have to practice moving beyond our neurology to access those resources of endurance, which is hard work that necessitates courage.

We can flourish during transitions when we believe past approaches have created a foundation of readiness for the next transition, and that those approaches can be adapted to better fit the next stage. When we come from a place of active curiosity, we can focus on learning about a new environment, and then incorporate the information and strategies that feel most helpful. When we do this, we tend to thrive in the early adjustment period of a new transition.

Values visioning

Levels of uncertainty vary from person to person and from situation to situation. Sometimes people know exactly what they want to do and what the next step is going to look like. Sometimes people are still clarifying what the next step is going to be. Either way, no one can know exactly what will happen. So, there is always a level of uncertainty associated with a next step. It is natural to become preoccupied with questions like, "How much money do I need to make?" "Should I relocate and where?" "What will my time commitment be?" "How can this job effect my future aspirations?" These questions are helpful to answer, but unchecked they can root us in expectation and aspects we don't control which can increase fear. Values visioning exercises can help us utilize our values relationship to project forward and manage the uncertainties associated with change.

For each of the following questions, pick a time period in the future (e.g., one month from now, six months from now, one year from now, five years from now) that best serves you and the visioning of a particular life role.

Work role

Think of your work role. What values do you hope to express and fulfill in this future work role?

In values visioning, it is important just to get a glimpse of these answers. The likelihood that you will be able to express these values is not important in this exercise. The purpose is developing awareness as to what values you hope to express in your work role. This pattern of thinking puts your values expression ahead of your fears and frustrations when assessing future work roles. This question is also helpful when we are at interview stages. When possible, we can better recognize environments that best allow us to express values that are important to us.

Leisure role

Tonya knew that the next few years would be invasive. She needed regular privacy to recharge, and this metalworking apprenticeship would not provide much alone time. However, in five years, when she planned on owning her own shop, she would have the privacy and autonomy over her time that she'd always wanted.

The design guild Tonya apprenticed at was a social type of environment. She regularly had to work in groups or with a mentor. The other employees were on the younger side and the bosses liked to hang out with everybody after work.

Tonya's experience at the guild would eventually be great for her resumé and building a client network, but the first year was exhausting. The daily work load, apprenticeship, and off-hour socializing with coworkers led Tonya to establish Sunday as an "alone day" for herself. She declined fishing trips, barbecues, and concerts with coworkers.

Her Sundays were spent alone in her room reading, watching TV, drawing, or cooking. There were still Sundays when she had to work or would occasionally agree to a social engagement. However, setting the intention to carve out a boundary for her privacy helped her manage the draining aspects of her time at the guild.

Seven years later, Tonya had her own shop and steady design jobs. It was the level of privacy and independence she'd always wanted. Now her Sundays were spent socializing and building relationships, and this was the desired amount of time she preferred spending with others.

The Leisure role is the portion of life outside of work where you have more autonomy over how you spend your time. It's not necessarily about being in a place of leisure. When you have more control over your time, what values do you want to express? This may not be very leisurely, but it is important for satisfying or planning to satisfy values that may not be expressed in your work life. In a future time period of your choosing, what values do you want to express in your leisure role? What would that look like? Why is it important for you to express those values?

We don't necessarily control the kind of work culture we are walking into. Values visioning with our leisure role can help us to manage periods of intensity at work. Having an idea of the values we want expressed in our leisure role gives us a stronger sense of agency and efficiency in the spare moments we do have.

Relationship role

What values will be important for you to express in important relationships in the future?

There are obvious answers like Belonging, but it is important to go deeper with this question. For example, "I want to be around people or with a person that will be okay with my devotion to Creativity." "I want to be with someone who will respect and affirm my Privacy value." "I'm going to be so overwhelmed with work that I want relationships that will allow me to unpack and figure out aspects of life." Think about important relationships or future friends, and share with your partner values you hope to express in a future time period.

Unplanned transitions

There are other types of transitions we deal with throughout our lives. Unplanned transitions are unexpected life changes. These may include losing a loved one, getting fired, dealing with illness, or an unanticipated increase in resources (e.g., inherited wealth) that may result in a significant life change. Unplanned transitions are particularly stressful because they may be unwanted and painful. They demand that we pause and reflect on the meaning of this change in our lives. A critical component of successfully navigating unplanned transitions is coping effectively.

As discussed in Chapter 9, It is important to devote significant time to coping with or recovering from unplanned change. Anger and depression are common reactions; we cope effectively when we honor these reactions instead of looking for immediate ways to "feel better". When people flourish, they honor their reactions, "I'm hurt because something hurtful happened," and they work to not draw conclusions. We can be personally conclusive when we're hurt: "See, I can't trust anybody." Those are honest conclusions and may even be accurate, but it can help to challenge any conclusions because we are filtering our thoughts through intense emotions that may influence misguided conclusions about our world, our future, and ourselves.

During coping periods, it is important to devote time to self-care strategies and values-based behavior, even if this doesn't make us feel better at the time. We are usually able to cope better with emotional storms if we feel that we are able to still commit some time to things that are important to us, even while affected. These steps can help us start to define ourselves beyond our grief, and find meaning in joining this difficult change with our life. Once we have recovered enough to trust our reflections and self-analysis, it may be helpful to clarify how this life change has affected what is important to us and evolve our relationship with our values.

Unexpected changes that involve increases of resources or attained outcomes can range from pleasant to overwhelming experiences. Despite possible improvements to our surroundings, we tend to be most fulfilled when our values align with our behavior. Taking time to develop our relationship with our values after such a transition can help align new behaviors with our values. Have certain values shifted in importance as a result of this transition? What do important values look like in action as healthy or unhealthy expressions after this change?

Internal transitions

Another transitional experience we encounter in our lives can be viewed as internal transition. These changes occur when our convictions about what is important shift as a result of learning, aging, powerful experiences, impact from others, etc. Some values may start to decrease in importance while others start taking a higher priority. We may be living according to behaviors that are no longer congruent to the values that have internally shifted. A healthy and evolving relationship with our values is needed to guide our behavior to align with what is transitioning to be meaningful. These changes are not easy and can often be overwhelming. We have to deal not only with realigning our behavior but also the reactions of others who may not understand or agree with the changes they are noticing in our behavior. It can be an intimidating process that requires strong commitment and courage to enact a change fostering greater integrity and self-esteem.

Key points

1. Life transitions can incite higher levels of uncertainty, which can cause natural responses such as control, avoidance, self-doubt, and an over-reliance on outcomes to reassure us that we made the right decision.
2. Planned or proactive transitions can benefit from values visioning exercises. These exercises utilize our values relationship to project forward at a time when we can be naturally preoccupied by fear-based expectations and aspects we don't control.
3. Other types of life changes are unplanned transitions, which necessitate healthy self-care and coping strategies, and internal transitions, which require courage and commitment to realign behaviors to reflect values that have shifted in importance.

Personalizing the concepts

1. Try to remember some of the answers from your values visioning questions, and when you get to that future stage, see how your experience coincides or differs from what you envisioned. What factors contributed to those similarities or differences?

References

Brown, D. (1995). A values-based approach to facilitating career transitions. *The Career Development Quarterly*, 44(1), 4–11.

Busacca, L.A. (2002). Career problem assessment: A conceptual schema for counselor training. *Journal of Career Development*, 29(2), 129–146.

Busacca, L., Beebe, R., & Toman, S. (2010). Life and work values of counselor trainees: A national survey. *The Career Development Quarterly*, 59(1), 2–18.

Clemens, E., & Milsom, A. (2008). Enlisted service members' transition into the civilian world of work: A cognitive information processing approach. *The Career Development Quarterly*, 56(3), 246–256.

Ercegovac, I., & Koludrovic, M. (2012). Life values and divorce: Intergeneration and family perspective. *Sociology and Space*, 50(2), 257–273.

Galassi, J.P., Crace, R.K., Martin, G.A., James, R., & Wallace, L. (1992). Client preferences and anticipations in career counseling: A preliminary investigation. *Journal of Counseling Psychology*, 39, 46–55.

Galassi, J.P., Martin, G.A., Crace, R.K., & James, R. (1992). Guiding assumptions, data, and minor pestilence. *Journal of Counseling Psychology*, 39, 66–70.

Notes

16 Leadership and team development

College scouts at a state basketball tournament weren't unusual, but the call from Coach Wright was. Coach Wright wasn't the type of guy who called coaches from an opposing team. Coach Richards was about half Coach Wright's age, and had quickly gained a reputation at a job she initially regarded as a stopgap. Gerry Richards' third knee surgery had ended her EuroLeague career. Recovering in her hometown, she hadn't thought of coaching basketball until a local High School asked her to fill in. Six years later, Richards had turned the local boys' High School team into one of the top squads in the state. She still didn't see herself as a traditional coach; in fact most players called her Gerry. But working and learning from the kids had provided a fulfillment she hadn't found while playing the sport.

Across the state, Coach Wright was an aging force in High School basketball. He couldn't understand how those college Athletic Directors could be looking at the flash-in-the-pan, female Coach Richards? A phone call was in order. "Look Coach Richards, the scouts at the tournament are gonna be lookin' at you more than the kids. You better be ready. If you blow this shot, you might not get another. I've been at the same High School for thirty years with five titles on my resumé."

"Thanks, Coach Wright, we're looking forward to playing you all next week."

"Be ready, Miss. 'Cause this ol' dog ain't gonna let you waltz into a college job without a fight."

"Understood."

A week later, Coach Wright had scheduled a shoot-around meeting the night before the tournament. Some players rushed to the shoot-around and some took their time, knowing Coach Wright would be late. Unfortunately, two players miscalculated and wound up arriving later than the coach. "Well, I'm glad you boys will be able to provide us with some entertainment. Pushups till ya puke!"

Coach Wright watched for several minutes until the players were exhausted, then turned to his team. "It's gonna hurt worse than that if you don't follow the simple plans I have for tomorrow. I gotta a lotta influence with those scouts. So, ya better impress me."

Coach Wright proceeded to outline an aggressive game plan that repeatedly contradicted itself. One of the players tried to clarify, "Sir, when do you want us to do the stagger screens?"

"If you can't remember a simple plan then you're gonna have to join the pushup crew!"

One of the players doing pushups began to cramp up and stopped.

"Y'all aren't tough... Everybody hit the floor. Forty pushups on my count. Y'all gotta trust me."

Across town, Coach Richards had also scheduled a meeting the night before the tournament. However, her team arrived five minutes before the scheduled shoot-around to find Coach Richards doing pushups.

"Quick workout, Gerry?"

"I gotta get rid of some of this nervous energy."

Some of the team joined Richards. "Alright, alright. Don't waste your energy. Tomorrow's gonna be intense."

The team settled in for a meeting as Richards began, "I don't want to build a bunch of concrete strategies that could knock you off your rhythm. You all are in the State Playoffs for a reason. The more you can focus on 'play' even though we're in a big college arena, the more high-percentage looks you'll get. Let's just lead with that."

Most of the team nodded along in agreement. However, one player argued, "Coach, I think we should do a little more planning. This is the biggest stage most of us have been on with scouts watching."

Richards allowed the point to resonate. She thought carefully as her perspective shifted. "How many of you feel pretty loose about tomorrow and how many are feeling a good amount of pressure? This isn't a test. Pressure's not a bad thing. You can be honest. Who feels pretty loose?"

Seven of the twelve players raised their hands. Three of the other five players who felt pressure were her best starters. Coach Richards addressed the three, "How about we start with a little bit of structure. Let's do two out and you three in motion. Just focus on basic shuffle offense assignments. And we'll do 1-3-1 zone for defense with you three in the lane. Jay you be chaser, Steve tail, and Carl king of the hill. Let's try that for a quarter and see if it loosens things up. Anybody feeling pressure who initially said they're feeling loose?"

Two of her tallest bench players raised their hands. "Ok, ya know what? Let's have Sean play mid and Danny tail for the first few minutes. Steve and Carl, no knock on you, but I think coming off the bench will help get rid of some butterflies."

One of the players spoke up, "Coach, do you mind if I say something?"

"Shoot."

"I liked your original idea of sticking to our rhythm without concrete plans."

"...Kevin, you might be right, but the more I think about it, the more I realize that this isn't a normal game. We're dealing with scouts, a big arena, and Coach Wright's gonna put out an aggressive team. So I think a little strategy to test the waters and provide a little direction could help. If it doesn't work, we can scrap it and go man to man or play small four-out situations."

"Ok... your instincts usually end up being right, anyway."

"They're our instincts, Kevin."

Most of today's effective leadership models espouse the central importance of values (Astin & Astin, 1996, 2000; Gentile, 2010). An important component of leadership is developing trust through integrity. In Part II of the Authentic Excellence program, we explored how values lead to a greater consciousness of self and link to our behavior. In Chapter 7 we learned how essential aligning your values to your behavior is for self-esteem and resilience. It is also a primary means of gaining respect and trust when you lead. There is no question that communication is an essential component of effective leadership. Communication helps provide clarity of purpose, mission, and goals. But the most effective leaders with the highest level of respect typically are very consistent in aligning their words and behavior with their values (Clercq, Fontaine, & Anseel, 2008; Zogmaister, Arcuri, Castelli, & Smith, 2008).

While many ego-driven leaders enjoy and embrace the power that comes with their leadership position, we've found that many effective values-centered leaders are slightly uncomfortable with the power of their positional leadership. Interestingly, these leaders tend not to leverage their authority when things get difficult or tense among teams. However, they find effectiveness in openly communicating the "why" behind what they do. They are decisive and don't shy away from their leadership responsibilities, but they don't mind being questioned about their decisions. They don't get defensive because they believe in the efficacy of being questioned and challenged. These effective leaders don't try to convince, but focus instead on describing decisions through a values lens. They allow for a diversity of emotion and opinion, and seek to understand the values lens of each team member. They incorporate the values of each individual into their goals, planning, and performance evaluations. These leaders are also open to differing perspectives having an impact on their own values, and they then communicate the "why" behind any shift in direction.

A common misstep that leaders make is incorporating a positional perspective to developing a team's core values. In other words, the team's values are reflective of the leader's values. While this can be effective if you have a healthy, flourishing leader, it can also serve to create a very judgmental culture by declaring what values are celebrated and what values are dismissed. If team members feel they need to hide values that are important to them because they are not aligned with the leader, that eventually impacts team effectiveness.

The following are team development exercises that utilize the LVI to encourage a non-positional values culture.

Assessing team values

Step 1: Have each team member clarify and assess their current relationship with their values. We recommend taking the free Life Values Inventory Online assessment (www.lifevaluesinventory.org) or utilizing the assessment in Appendix A. (Note to Team Leaders: Life Values Inventory Online provides a free-to-the-public feature that generates anonymous aggregate reports of a group's Values Profiles.)

Step 2: Spend time at a retreat or in staff meetings sharing individual values results using the questions from Chapter 6. It's optimal to share in pairs/dyads and rotate partners throughout the questions. This develops a greater sense of understanding and respect for each team member through a values lens.

Step 3: Create 14 stations using the 14 values of the LVI. Have all team members go to the station of their #1 ranked value in their High Priority category at the same time, have everybody take time to notice where team members are stationed, then have all team members go to their #2 ranked value station, and so on. Encourage team members to be curious as to how other members move throughout the values stations. Some individuals may go to unexpected values. Many people may go to some values and few may go to others. Prompt and allow questions, comments, and conversations. Advise them to refrain from using the word "why" because it can connote judgment (e.g., "Why do you value that?"). Instead, phrases like "tell me more" can be effective. "Tell me more about how that value became important to you," or "Tell me more about what it's like to have that as a high value in your life." If time allows, go through some of the values in other categories like Over-Attention, Under-Attention, and Medium/Low Priority. This exercise allows team members to see the diversity of values that may exist within the team.

Step 4: Discuss, as a team, the group's Values Profile. (A collective aggregate can be generated through the Life Values Inventory Online aggregate feature. You can also keep a tally of the number of people that stand at each value as team members move through Step 3.) You will often see a cluster of values naturally emerge from the group profile. There is no set number of values a team should have as their collective values; it just depends on whether the values have group-level endorsement. It can also be helpful to see if there are any significant group patterns for the Over-Attention, Under-Attention, and Medium/Low Priority values.

Step 5: Based on the High Priority team values, discuss the strengths of those values and what they look like in action in the context of daily team functioning. Identify both healthy and unhealthy actions that stem from those values. Discuss any challenges associated with your team values and steps to manage those challenges. During this time, it is important for supervisors to invite individuals to observe and comment on how their individual values are similar and dissimilar to the group profile, and how they manage both the congruency and differences. This normalizes and affirms diversity while encouraging open conversation and thought about how to healthfully express and manage diverse values.

Step 6: As a team, develop an Integrity Statement that summarizes the team's Values Profile and how others would preferably see your team's behavior as a result of those values. The Integrity Statement should be brief, action-oriented, and congruent with team values without being overly idealistic. Use the Integrity Statement along with your mission statement to develop goals and visioning for the coming year. Reassess the team's values and corresponding steps each year.

Step 7: As leaders, supervisory meetings with employees should include open discussions of how their individual Values Profiles are and are not aligned with the group's Values Profile. Rather than being a time of judgment, it provides an open opportunity for thought and discussion about how their values can be healthfully expressed and managed at work and in other life roles.

Key points

1. The individual values work of the Authentic Excellence program can be applied to the context of team development and leadership.
2. Leaders who align their behavior with their values and create an atmosphere of open and diverse inclusion of individual team member values can experience consistent team productivity, fulfillment, and resilience.
3. Leaders can utilize the LVI and other values-centered work to develop awareness and trust among team members.

Personalizing the concepts

1. How does your individual values profile compare to your team's profile? What factors contribute to similarities and differences?
2. How, when, and where can you express important individual values that are not part of your team's values within and outside of your work setting?

References

Astin, A.W., & Astin, H.S. (1996). *A social change model of leadership development: Guidebook, version 3.* Los Angeles, CA: UCLA Higher Education Research Institute.

Astin, A.W., & Astin, H.S. (2000). *Leadership reconsidered: Engaging higher education in social change.* Battle Creek, MI: W.K. Kellogg Foundation.

Clercq, S., Fontaine, J., & Anseel, F. (2008). In search of a comprehensive value model for assessing supplementary person-organization fit. *The Journal of Psychology*, 142(3), 277–302.

Gentile, M.C. (2010). *Giving voice to values: How to speak your mind when you know what's right.* New Haven, CT: Yale University Press.

Zogmaister, C., Arcuri, L., Castelli, L., & Smith, E.R. (2008). The impact of loyalty and equality on implicit ingroup favoritism. *Group Processes & Intergroup Relations*, 11(4), 493–512.

Notes

17 Decision-making and values

"So I took the job."

"What job?"

"That job I told you about last week."

"Isn't that job in another state?"

"Yeah."

"You didn't wanna talk it over with me or anything?"

"I told you about it last week."

"You mentioned it last week and haven't talked about it since. I even asked you a couple of days ago, 'What happened with that offer?' And you said, 'I dunno.'"

"Because I didn't want to think about it."

"And you just woke up today and decided to accept a job in another state?"

"I was checking to see if they'd offered it to someone else, and when they said they hadn't, I jumped at it."

"We'd have to move."

"Do you not want to do this?"

Ilya was getting frustrated with the recent challenges of her three-year relationship with James. After a night of arguing, Ilya heard James talking on the phone with his mother.

"What did your mom say about the job?"

"I didn't tell her."

"Why?"

"I didn't want to make her upset if she didn't like my decision."

"Do you even like your decision?"

"I need a job. I can't turn down an offer when I don't have other options."

"You don't have other options right now, but you might later."

"You're mad because I didn't talk it over with you."

"Of course."

"I'm sorry. I should've talked to you before agreeing, but I looked at my bank account yesterday and panicked. It's not like I've made good decisions when I do talk about it ad nauseam."

"Your last job was a good decision. It's not your fault the company got bought out."

Ilya spent the next several days deciding if she was going to move with James or not. She consulted her sister.

"Do you want to move?"

"Honestly, I kinda do, but I'm upset that he just assumed I would."

"Did you tell him that?"

"Of course."

"So what are you gonna do?"

"I made this list of reasons to stay and reasons to end the relationship."

"A pros and cons list?"

"No, a little more involved than that because I came up with more reasons to leave than to stay… but the reasons to stay are more probable and important to me."

"Like what?"

"It really comes down to this: I'm concerned about him growing. He's insecure when it comes to jobs and his family, but I've seen him grow in the past when I didn't think he would. He reached a breaking point with some of his friends, the partying, and he completely turned things around. When he makes up his mind, he commits."

"But he has to reach a breaking point?"

"That's what I'm worried about, but the more I think about it, the more probable it is that he will get fed up with being insecure and make a change. It's not like he's unaware. He'll admit when he's off track."

"That's big."

"I know, and I think it overshadows the reasons to break up… It'd be nice to be alone, though… focus on my career. What do ya think I should do?"

"Honestly, one choice is not more right than the other. I think you can make both work well for you. Breaking up will hurt, but it will allow you to focus on your own life. On the other hand, it's important to have a partner that can see when they're off center. He's proven he's not afraid to work on himself, and he treats you well."

"Yeah… when you have two rights, they both feel wrong."

Undecided versus indecisive: Avoiding the plateau effect when making decisions

Because values are basic beliefs that guide our behavior, they are an important part of our decision-making process. In Part I, we analyzed the Fear-Based Model of Excellence and how a plateau effect can occur when we develop patterns of dealing with fear and pressure through avoidance and over-control. Eventually this model inhibits our effectiveness when acting on important values. The same vulnerability can occur when making important decisions. Generally speaking, you want to make decisions that are aligned with your prioritized values. But life is not always that clear. What do you do when you're trying to decide between two or more "right" decisions?

When we have opportunities that put us in a situation where we feel like we're having to choose between two important values, we can drift into a place of undecidedness or indecision. There is a difference between being undecided and indecisive. Undecided means we need more information to make an informed decision. Indecision stems from the fear of making the wrong decision. Fear can also influence undecidedness. We can become too thorough in our search for information that it starts to become a form of avoidance. Indecision can lead to two ineffective patterns of decision-making: over-commitment and avoidance. It's hard to say "no" to an opportunity that speaks to our values, and it is natural to fear making a "wrong" decision. Furthermore, a common fear among young adults is the Fear of Missing Out. As a result, we can agree to too many opportunities, which leads to over-commitment and eventual burnout. We can also avoid making decisions until the moment when we absolutely have to decide, and then hope that the decision turns out well.

How do we avoid these pitfalls when it comes to decision-making?

Decision-Making (DM) Tip 1: Clarify how any of your values influence your decision-making style. For example, Independence and Interdependence are particularly common factors in determining decisions. People who have a highly prioritized Independence value are likely to make their own decisions with little reference to others. Individuals who have a highly prioritized Interdependence value are likely to weigh up the opinions of their family or the wishes of significant others when they make decisions. Many people have both Independence and Interdependence as highly prioritized values. When this occurs, individuals may choose to do what is independently more right for them, but will also consider others' opinions strongly before making their final decision.

DM Tip 2: When choosing between opportunities that can reward two different values, focus on prioritization. When we are trying to decide between two "rights", we can be hindered by the ambivalence or guilt that comes with having to forsake one value for another. When faced with that difficulty, it is important to courageously prioritize your values for each situation. For a particular decision, which value matters more, even if it is only slightly more? Accept that a part of you will feel ambivalent because the value you don't prioritize higher will whisper to your conscience that you may be making the wrong decision. Collect relevant information to understand the opportunity, prioritize your values for only the current situation, and courageously trust your prioritization.

DM Tip 3: To avoid over-commitment and burnout, allow a 24-hour pause before agreeing to any opportunity. Even if you immediately know your decision, it can help to say something like, "It sounds like a great opportunity. Can I get back to you tomorrow?" During those 24 hours, ask yourself two questions: "What meaning does this opportunity provide for me?" and "At what cost?" We tend not to ask the second question. It feels wrong to say "no" to any opportunity that speaks to our values, so we will often say "yes" by default and assume that we'll find the time and energy somewhere. Instead, assume that you are 100% committed and that if you are going to take on something new, something will have to be reduced or eliminated. Being thoughtful about the costs of a new opportunity allows us to prioritize our values and manage the fear of saying "no". If you believe the costs outweigh the meaning at this point in time, courageously decline the opportunity, trusting that other opportunities will present themselves in the future.

DM Tip 4: Rather than do a simple cost/benefit or pros and cons analysis, add a little values texture to the process. First, pick one side of a decision as if you were going to go in that direction. Second, list the reasons and factors that move you toward that side of the decision. Third, list the reasons and factors that would move you away from that side of the decision. Fourth, rate each of the factors that you listed from 1–5 based on how important each factor is to you at this point in time. Fifth, rate each factor from 1–5 based on how probable and realistic that factor is. This process can help highlight patterns that will help your decision. For instance, you may have more factors listed that would move you away from the decision but the factors that move you toward it are rated higher in importance. Or you may notice that several of the factors that cause you to move away from that decision are more fear-based and not very probable (e.g., "My friends will leave me." "My family will disown me." "What if I get 10 years down the road and find out it was a terrible mistake?").

DM Tip 5: Once you make a decision, own it for the sake of resilience. Our language around a decision can influence this process. Listen to your language and notice how many times you say, "I have to…" "I need to…" "I can't…" When we use these phrases, we're leading with fear and not owning our decisions. It can help to change our perspective to use language like "It's right for me to…" "I choose to…" "I choose not to…" "I will…" "I won't…" The very slight change from, "I have to work on this paper that is due at noon," to, "It's right for me to work on this paper that is due at noon," can mean the difference between resentment and resilience.

DM Tip 6: Judge the worth of a decision by the process of the decision-making, not by the future outcomes. At the time we make a decision, we don't know how things will work out in the future, and there are many factors beyond your control that could influence future outcomes. Hence, it doesn't help us to judge the worth of a decision by something that happens in the future. To flourish, we must courageously go through a thoughtful, values-driven process of decision-making and then commit to that decision. If you find yourself going in a different direction down the line, it doesn't mean that your previous decision was wrong. It means you have more information to make another values-based decision.

Key points

1. It is difficult to make decisions that align with our values when we have to choose between two "right" decisions.
2. There is a difference between being undecided and indecisive.
3. Five tips to manage the difficulty of making effective, values-based decisions are:
   a. Clarify how your values influence your decision-making style.
   b. Allow a 24-hour pause before agreeing to any opportunity.
   c. Focus on prioritization of values.
   d. Rate factors on both sides of a decision based on importance and realistic probability.
   e. Once you make a decision, own it for the sake of resilience.
   f. Judge the worth of a decision by the process of the decision-making, not by the future outcomes.

Personalizing the concepts

1. How do the values of Independence and Interdependence currently influence your decision-making? What other important values influence your decision-making process (e.g., Objective Analysis, Creativity, Belonging, Spirituality, etc.)?
2. Think of a time when you felt good about a decision you made because of the process rather than the outcomes that resulted from that decision. What were the factors that made the process work?
3. Think of a time when you felt bad about a decision-making process. What factors involving that process didn't work?

Notes

18 Conclusion

Redefining authenticity, trust, and compassion

"You're not upset about moving back home?"

"Mom needs my help."

"Your brother can take care of her. You can't give up everything you've been working for."

"I'm always going to be involved in finance… predicting the market, studying trends."

"Yeah but the firm loves you and you've only been working there for six months."

"It'll give me more time to research. That's what I prefer doing anyway."

"Terry… what if something happens to your mom? You'll have no career to fall back on. You'll have to start from square one."

"…I'm going to have to handle that devastation. I care about family, my friends, finance… I'll create something from there."

"I wish I had your confidence."

"It's not confidence. I'm just sticking to what I know about myself."

"You know more about yourself than most."

"So do you."

"I know my landlord is threatening to kick me out."

"For playing drums?"

"Yeah, and it's just my electronic kit. I can't believe everybody in the building has a problem with it."

"You can't practice drums in your studio apartment."

"I need to play drums."

"Not in a studio apartment."

"I found a practice space, but it's expensive."

"Well, at least you'll have somewhere to play."

"But now I have to pick up more shifts to pay for the space, and I can only practice Monday, Wednesday, and Friday…"

"Why don't you focus on other aspects of your music while you can't play drums as much?"

"I need to play drums."

"I know, but what about practicing stick technique or researching different rhythm books… Find your voice while you can't play your kit."

"Terry, I need to play drums."

"Why is 'playing drums' limited to playing your kit in a sound-proofed room?"

"I don't know advanced rhythm theory or proper stick technique."

"Then take this time to learn."

"I don't want a book telling me that I can't play"

"Only you can make a book say that… Why do you like playing drums?"

"The energy release, the music… I dunno, I love it."

"Then trust that source. You can find new ways to exert that creative energy and play music."

"Yeah, but not like I can when I play drums."

"Then maybe playing less is a good challenge because it can force you to grow in different ways that may strengthen your music."

"Maybe, but… Terry, are you really looking at the challenge of moving home as an opportunity to grow?"

"No, not entirely. I'm choosing to move home because my family needs me and I trust that I'll make it work. The challenge will filter what I know about myself into a new direction."

"What if I don't want to go in a new direction?"

"That's okay as long as you're not afraid to go in a new direction. Trust yourself."

Redefining authenticity

When we're stuck at good and not flourishing, we tend to think of authenticity as being our natural selves. When we equate being genuine to our natural self, we are relating authenticity to our current emotions and natural coping patterns. But that's only a surface level of authenticity. A deeper form of authenticity is aligning our responses to our values and healthy coping patterns. So, if someone upsets me, and I don't react with anger because it's more in line with my values to interact in a respectful manner, that's a deeper form of authenticity, rather than a fake reaction. Or if I process anger by assertively expressing my objection to a violation that has occurred in an effort to correct the issue or establish boundaries, that is a deeper form of authenticity rather than reactive emotionality. When we're upset because of a personal values violation, it's natural for us to follow that path of upset towards the nobility of our rightness. But that path can also cause us to justify our natural, reactive way of expressing upset emotions. It's important to work on healthy coping patterns so that we manage our emotions in an effective manner, both for our health and to be interpersonally effective. If I have habitually expressed anger through rage, then it is easy for me to step into that rage even if I have a values-based intention to correct a wrong that has occurred. But if I know that the healthiest way for me to cope with anger is to take some time for myself so that I can gain perspective, I'm not being fake or ignoring the values violation, I am reflecting a deeper level of authenticity. Bringing healthy coping patterns into the equation of values expression when upset can move us beyond the pure motivation to respond to a values violation and factor in the impact of our behavior. It allows us to sensitively step into difficult conversations because we are open enough to consider the impact of our actions on others and healthfully consider how to be most effective in our communication. As we develop a relationship with our values and train toward an expressive mindset, we can notice a shift from our natural selves to one's deeper authentic self. Over time, this authentic self starts to emerge as a new natural self where our reactions to things around us are more reflective of our values than of our mood.

Redefining trust and compassion: The core of flourishing and resilience

The Five Paradigm Shifts are designed to develop a highly refined sense of two things: trust and compassion (see Figure 18.1). But we describe trust and compassion in a manner that is different from how we typically think of the terms.

Trust

A colleague, Gary Glass, contributes to an important idea involving the relationship between vulnerability and authentic excellence: "What is the opposite of control? Most people say chaos." However, an answer we

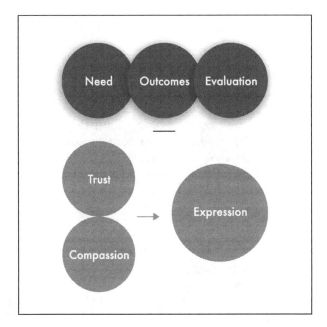

Figure 18.1 Plateau versus Authentic Excellence

find more indicative of authentic excellence is that the opposite of control is trust. The problem is that to get to an authentic level of trust and understanding you have to go through a period of vulnerability. We naturally don't like vulnerability because of three fears: the fear of being hurt, the fear of getting played, and the fear of being perceived as weak. We can avoid vulnerability, which keeps us from developing trust or stay in a place of control, but this is misleading because we don't control a large portion of the world around us.

You've demonstrated your ability to be vulnerable by going through the work of the Five Paradigm Shifts. Developing a relationship with your values, aligning your behavior with what is important to you, managing fear differently, building confidence in effective coping strategies, and fostering an expressive mindset all involves vulnerability which leads to trust.

This form of trust is not how society typically defines it. "Just trust that things will turn out okay." That's passive trust. The active trust that flourishing work leads to is so important because trust is what overrides fear.

Active trust and Authentic Excellence are defined as:

1. "I trust that I know what my personal truth is" (meaning that you know your values and your current relationship with them).
2. "I trust that I know what my truth looks like in action" (how your values manifest themselves in the course of a day).
3. "I trust that when life is hard, harsh, or unfair I know how to manage the challenges in a healthy way."

Compassion

Compassion overrides evaluation. But the form of compassion we are referring to is not how our society typically defines it. "Just love others." The compassion that leads to flourishing is a commitment to active curiosity, to learning instead of judgment. Active curiosity is a skill that fosters empathy toward yourself and others. We can often be more compassionate to others than we are to ourselves. We are often our harshest critics, and there can be a misconception that compassion toward ourselves bypasses accountability. However, compassion can lead to deep self-accountability because when active curiosity replaces judgment we're not threatened by analysis, which promotes learning and in turn growth.

Compassion overrides evaluation, and trust overrides fear. Those two components lead to living a life of expression (see Figure 18.1). It takes work, but it's work you've done throughout Parts I and II. You've practiced flourishing by trusting and being actively curious. Continuing this practice doesn't have to be deeply reflective all the time. The Action Plan is designed to provide a focused outline for daily practice.

Distilled practice

We believe the Dynamic Blueprinting Action Plan is the optimal process for internalizing the Five Paradigm Shifts. However, there are times when the Action Plan may feel too extensive or overwhelming. It is important not to focus too much on the concepts to the point of inaction. Self-awareness can be intriguing but we can easily avoid the work necessary to move from insight to practice.

If for any reason you find yourself struggling to utilize or regularly commit to your Action Plan, bring back the principle of volitional confidence: "What of this can I do?" Distill the process down to a practice that is more conducive to consistent action. The following are two approaches that may help you get started.

Distilled Strategy A: Three-step daily practice

Answer the following question: If you could only be remembered for two things, and if you could only be remembered for your behavior, not your words, what would those two things be? This could be something that someone remembers you for after only spending a week with you. What do you hope people most remember you for, if it could only be two things?

For eight weeks, practice the following three daily steps. (1) Start each day by asking yourself, "What opportunities are there to practice the two things I most want to be remembered for?" One day you may only be able to practice those two things for a few minutes. Another day you may be able to spend all day expressing those two things. (2) Engage in the day with full experiential acceptance. (3) At the end of the day, take time to appreciate when and how you practiced those two things, with no "buts" allowed. At the end of those eight weeks, what do you notice about your mindset and effectiveness?

Distilled Strategy B: Four-step daily mindset

If you are more philosophical in your approach to life, consider the following four-step philosophy or mindset to approaching your day.

1. Show up.
2. Show up with courage and your values.
3. Define your success by the expression of your values.
4. When the world rewards your expression with positive outcomes, celebrate that as a great day, but not the new standard. When the world is harsh or unfair despite your values-based expression, focus on self-care. Then re-commit to showing up tomorrow with your courage and values.

Key points

1. As you move through the training program, your personal definition of authenticity can shift from the natural self that equates genuineness to emotion and natural coping patterns to a deeper authentic self that is defined by your values and healthy coping patterns.
2. Trust overrides fear, and compassion overrides evaluation. We have to go through a period of vulnerability to develop trust. We have to maintain a sense of active curiosity to replace judgment and develop compassion toward others and ourselves.

Notes

Appendix A: Life Values Inventory

LifeValues Inventory
CLARIFYING YOUR   PERSONAL TRUTH

R. Kelly Crace, Ph.D. & Duane Brown, Ph.D.

Developed by:

R. Kelly Crace, Ph.D. & Duane Brown, Ph.D.

Applied Psychology Resources, Inc.
Psychological Consulting, Counseling and Educational Resources

For more information on how to use your values for personal development
please visit www.lifevaluesinventory.org

Instructions

Values are beliefs that influence people's behavior and decision making. For example, if people believe that telling the truth is very important, they will try to be truthful when they deal with other people. Research has shown that understanding our values is one of the most important factors in determining satisfaction in our work, relationships, and leisure activities. All healthy personal values have a social context and, therefore, a certain level of societal "should" or moral weight associated with them. The reason for our focus on personal values has to do with the process of clarifying one's authenticity through a values lens. We believe if a person can accurately assess what truly matters to them at various times in their life and discern how those values can be healthfully expressed and managed in their behavior, then they are more equipped to understand and manage the relationship between their personal values and societally-weighted moral values. The Life Values Inventory is designed to help you clarify and prioritize your values and serve as a blueprint for future decision making.

On the following pages is a list of beliefs that guides people's behavior and helps them make important decisions. Read each one and then choose the response (1-5) that best describes how often the belief guides your behavior. Before you begin, complete the following practice item by circling the number that best describes how this belief guides your behavior now.

	...GUIDES MY BEHAVIOR:				
	Seldom	Sometimes		Frequently	
Being Healthy	1	2	3	4	5

If a belief in being healthy seldom guides your behavior, circle 1. If being healthy frequently guides your behavior, circle 5. If the best answer for you is between 1 and 5, circle the number (2, 3, or 4) that most accurately describes how this belief guides your behavior.

Read each item carefully and circle only one response. Usually your first idea is the best indicator of how you feel. Answer every item. There are no right or wrong answers. Your choices should describe your own values, not the values of others.

Important tips:

(1) All of the items reflect positive values. Avoid rating all items as 4 or 5. Use your behavior as a guide to your ratings.

(2) When thinking about your current behavior, think in terms of this general time in your life, not in terms of today or this past week.

Values Items

Add up your ratings for each three-item grouping and write the sum in the "Score" column. The letters (A, B, C, etc.) correlate to each of the **14 life values**, which will make up your "Values Profile" on the following page.

Example:

					2+3+4
Challenging myself to achieve	1	2	③	4	5
Improving my performance	1	2	3	④	5
Working hard to do better	1	②	3	4	5

→ 9 A

Page 4 ▸ Values Profile ▸ A ▸ Achievement *(Score)* ▸ 9

	...GUIDES MY BEHAVIOR:				Score
	Seldom	Sometimes	Frequently		
Challenging myself to achieve	1	2	3	4	5
Improving my performance	1	2	3	4	5
Working hard to do better	1	2	3	4	5
					A
Being liked by others	1	2	3	4	5
Being accepted by others	1	2	3	4	5
Feeling as though I belong	1	2	3	4	5
					B
Protecting the environment	1	2	3	4	5
Preserving nature	1	2	3	4	5
Appreciating the beauty of nature	1	2	3	4	5
					C
Being sensitive to others' needs	1	2	3	4	5
Helping others	1	2	3	4	5
Being concerned about the rights of others	1	2	3	4	5
					D
Coming up with new ideas	1	2	3	4	5
Being creative	1	2	3	4	5
Discovering new things or ideas	1	2	3	4	5
					E
Having financial success	1	2	3	4	5
Making money	1	2	3	4	5
Being wealthy	1	2	3	4	5
					F
Taking care of my body	1	2	3	4	5
Being in good physical shape	1	2	3	4	5
Being athletic	1	2	3	4	5
					G

Values Items
(Continued)

	...GUIDES MY BEHAVIOR:					Score	
	Seldom	Sometimes	Frequently				
Downplaying compliments or praise	1	2	3	4	5		
Being quiet about my successes	1	2	3	4	5		H
Avoiding credit for my accomplishments	1	2	3	4	5		
Being independent	1	2	3	4	5		
Giving my opinion	1	2	3	4	5		I
Having control over my time	1	2	3	4	5		
Accepting my place in my family or group	1	2	3	4	5		
Respecting the traditions of my family or group	1	2	3	4	5		J
Making decisions with my family or group in mind	1	2	3	4	5		
Relying on objective facts	1	2	3	4	5		
Relying on logic to solve problems	1	2	3	4	5		K
Being analytical	1	2	3	4	5		
Having time to myself	1	2	3	4	5		
Having quiet time to think	1	2	3	4	5		L
Having a private place to go	1	2	3	4	5		
Being reliable	1	2	3	4	5		
Being trustworthy	1	2	3	4	5		M
Meeting my obligations	1	2	3	4	5		
Believing in a higher power	1	2	3	4	5		
Believing there is something greater than ourselves	1	2	3	4	5		N
Living in harmony with my spiritual beliefs	1	2	3	4	5		

Values Profile

Scores			Rankings
A.	_____	**ACHIEVEMENT**	_____
		It is important to challenge myself and to work hard to improve.	
B.	_____	**BELONGING**	_____
		It is important to be accepted by others and to feel included.	
C.	_____	**CONCERN FOR THE ENVIRONMENT**	_____
		It is important to protect and preserve the environment.	
D.	_____	**CONCERN FOR OTHERS**	_____
		The wellbeing of others and helping others are important.	
E.	_____	**CREATIVITY**	_____
		It is important to have new ideas, create new things, or be creatively expressive.	
F.	_____	**FINANCIAL PROSPERITY**	_____
		It is important to be financially successful.	
G.	_____	**HEALTH AND ACTIVITY**	_____
		It is important to be healthy and physically active.	
H.	_____	**HUMILITY**	_____
		It is important to be humble and modest about my accomplishments.	
I.	_____	**INDEPENDENCE**	_____
		It is important to have a sense of autonomy with my decisions and actions.	
J.	_____	**INTERDEPENDENCE**	_____
		The expectations of my family, social group, team or organization are important.	
K.	_____	**OBJECTIVE ANALYSIS**	_____
		It is important to use logical principles to understand and solve problems.	
L.	_____	**PRIVACY**	_____
		It is important to have time alone.	
M.	_____	**RESPONSIBILITY**	_____
		It is important to be dependable and trustworthy.	
N.	_____	**SPIRITUALITY**	_____
		It is important to have spiritual beliefs that reflect being a part of something greater than myself.	

RANKINGS. You have completed the first step of values clarification by rating individual items on pages 2 & 3. The second step is to rank the 14 life values scales. Use your scores listed above as a guide to rank the values that are most important and influence your behavior. Begin the process by identifying your most important life value that frequently guides your behavior and place a "1" in the right column labeled "Rankings" by that value. Then identify your second most important value, your third, and so forth. At the end of this process, you should have assigned all of the values listed above a number ranging from 1-14. You may find it difficult to rank a few values because of tied scores or because they are so close in importance. In this instances, use your current behavior as a guide to let you know what values are currently the most influential.

Preferred Values Expression

Aligning Behavior with Desired Values

As you review the values profile of your current behavior, you may want to make a few adjustments in how you devote your time and energy. Look carefully at your values rankings on page 4. Thinking of the next six months to a year, what changes in your behavior would you like to make? Be realistic in your adjustments. Remember that you only have so many hours in a day and that your current environment may impact how much you can adjust your devotion of time and energy.

The four categories below each represent a different relationship between the importance you place on a value and how much attention (time and energy) you devote to it.

Looking at your values rankings on page 4, select the category that *best* fits each value.

High Priority	Over-Attention	Under-Attention	Low Priority
Values in this category are important to me AND I frequently act on them.	I am focusing on these values more than I would prefer.	I am not focusing on these values as much as I would prefer.	These values are less important and I don't act on them very frequently.

Preferred Values Expression

Where you Express your Values:
Values & Life Roles

We express our values through our life roles. Since it is rare that one life role, such as work, satisfies all of our values, we often devote time and energy to several roles. While we may be involved in many activities and relationships, most people divide their time into three major life roles: (1) Work/Academics; (2) Important Relationships; and (3) Leisure/Community Activities. **Using the values on page 4, list the values you hope to have satisfied in each of these three life roles.**

You can list a value in more than one role. If there is another important role that doesn't fit under the other three role categories, list that value under 'Other' and notate that other life role. If you do not want to devote time and energy to a value, write that value under the 'Limited or No Expression' category.

Work/Academics	Important Relationships	Leisure/Community Activities

Other	Limited or No Expression

Appendix B: Dynamic Blueprinting Action Plan

DYNAMIC BLUEPRINTING
Values Expression Action Plan

—

This guide is intended as a reference for how your values look in action. It's not another "to do" list. Let it serve as a reminder that the **worth** of your day is based on your expression of values, while outcomes reflect only the **mood** of the day.

YOUR VALUES IN ACTION

Values	Healthy Expression	Unhealthy Expression

DYNAMIC BLUEPRINTING
Values Expression Action Plan

Fear Management Strategy:

Coping/Self-Care Strategies & Training:

Developing the Expressive Mindset

1. What is the ***most right*** devotion of my time and energy today?
2. When feeling, "I can't," ask, "What of this can I do?" Then imagine doing so.
3. Expression of talent and energy with full acceptance of the experience.
4. Appreciation of what I did and why.
5. What is one thing I can learn from today that will help me tomorrow?

Training Tips

1. Change your personal language
   Replace "have to, need to, can't" with...
       "will/won't, choose to/not to, it's right for me to/not to".
   Replace "right but hard" with "hard but right" or "right and only hard".
2. Before committing to an opportunity, ask yourself...
   "At what value?" and of equal importance, "At what cost?"
3. Review this Action Plan weekly (daily during the first week).
4. Read your Values Profile (generated from your LVI assessment) monthly
   and note what speaks to you at that time.

Appendix C: Life Values Inventory (LVI) references and previous publications

Allen, D. (2008). *Career maturity and college persistence: A longitudinal study of first-year students* (Doctoral dissertation). Retrieved from ProQuest Dissertations and Theses.

Almeida, L., & Pinto H.R. (2004). Life Values Inventory (LVI): Portuguese adaptation studies. *Canadian Journal of Career Development*, 3(1), 28–34.

Almeida, L, & Tavares, P. (2008). Life Values Inventory: Studies with Portuguese college students. International Journal of Psychology, 43(3–4), 484.

Ambler, V.M., Crace, R.K., & Fisler, J. (2015). Nurturing genius: Positive psychology as a framework for organization and practice. About Campus, 19, 24–28.

Bartels, K. (1995). *Psychosocial predictors of adjustment to the first year of college: A comparison of first-generation and second-generation students* (Doctoral dissertation). Retrieved from ProQuest Dissertations and Theses.

Barva, C. (1998). *The development of potential in high-achieving women* (Doctoral dissertation). Retrieved from ProQuest Dissertations and Theses.

Boyar, S. (2002). *A model of work and family conflict: The impact of work/family centrality and family role configuration on the demand–conflict relationship* (Doctoral dissertation). Retrieved from ProQuest Dissertations and Theses.

Brown, D. (1995). A values-based approach to facilitating career transitions. The Career Development Quarterly, 44(1), 4–11.

Brown, D. (2002). The role of work and cultural values in occupational choice, satisfaction, and success: A theoretical statement. *Journal of Counseling and Development*, 80(1), 48–56.

Brown, D., & Crace, R.K. (1996). *Life Values Inventory: Manual and user's guide.* Chapel Hill, NC: Life Values Resources.

Brown, D., & Crace, R.K. (1996). *Life Values Inventory: Occupations locator.* Chapel Hill, NC: Life Values Resources.

Brown, D., & Crace, R.K. (1996). Values in life role choices and outcomes: A conceptual model. The Career Development Quarterly, 44(3), 211–223.

Brown, D., & Crace, R.K. (1997). *Life Values Inventory: Educational majors locator.* Chapel Hill, NC: Life Values Resources.

Brown, D., & Crace, R.K. (1997). *Life Values Inventory: Leisure activities locator.* Chapel Hill, NC: Life Values Resources.

Brown, D., & Crace, R.K. (2002). *Facilitator's guide to the Life Values Inventory* (Revised ed.). Williamsburg, VA: Applied Psychology Resources.

Brown, D., & Crace, R.K. (2008). Brown's values-based career theory. In F.T. Leong (Ed.), *Encyclopedia of counseling* (Vol. 3). Thousand Oaks, CA: Sage.

Brown, D., Crace, R.K., & Almeida, L. (2006). A culturally sensitive, values-based approach to career counseling. In A.J. Palmo, W.J. Weikel, & D.P. Borsos (Eds.), *Foundations of mental health counseling* (3rd ed., pp. 144–171). Springfield, IL: Charles C. Thomas.

Busacca, L.A. (2002). Career problem assessment: A conceptual schema for counselor training. *Journal of Career Development*, 29(2), 129–146.

Busacca, L.A., Beebe, R., & Toman, S. (2010). Life and work values of counselor trainees: A national survey. *The Career Development Quarterly*, 59(1), 2–18.

Careers Forum (2005). *Australian Journal of Career Development*, 14(1), 67–81.

Cheng, A.-S. (2012). *Values in the net neutrality debate: Applying content analysis to testimonies from public hearings* (Doctoral dissertation). Retrieved from ProQuest Dissertations and Theses.

Cheng, A.-S., & Fleischmann, K. (2010). Developing a meta-inventory of human values. *Proceedings of the Association for Information Science and Technology*, 47(1), 1–10.

Cicirelli, V.G, Maclean, A.P., & Cox, L.S. (2000). Hastening death: A comparison of two end-of-life decisions. *Death Studies*, 24(5), 401–419.

Clemens, E., & Milsom, A. (2008). Enlisted service members' transition into the civilian world of work: A cognitive information processing approach. The Career Development Quarterly, 56(3), 246–256.

Clercq, S., Fontaine, J., & Anseel, F. (2008). In search of a comprehensive value model for assessing supplementary person-organization fit. *The Journal of Psychology*, 142(3), 277–302.

Cohen-Mansfield, J., Droge, J.A., & Bilig, N. (1992). Factors influencing hospital patients' preferences in the utilization of life-sustaining treatments. *The Gerontologist*, 32(1), 89–95.

Crace, R.K. (1992). *The development of an instrument to empirically assess life values* (Doctoral dissertation). Retrieved from ProQuest Dissertations and Theses.

Crace, R.K. (1996). Reflections on winning and optimal performance. *Performance Edge: The Letter of Performance Psychology*, 5(5), 1–8.

Crace, R.K. (2007). *The Praestare Project: An online mini-course for values clarification and personal development* (www.lifevaluesinventory.org). Williamsburg, VA: Applied Psychology Resources.

Crace, R.K. (2012). *Life Values Inventory Online* (www.lifevaluesinventory. org). Durham, NC: Life Values Inventory Online, Inc.

Crace, R.K., & Brown, D. (1996). *Life Values Inventory.* Chapel Hill, NC: Life Values Resources.

Crace, R.K., & Brown, D. (1996). *Understanding your values.* Chapel Hill, NC: Life Values Resources.

Crace, R.K., & Brown, D. (1997). *Life Values Inventory: User's guide.* Chapel Hill, NC: Life Values Resources.

Crace, R.K., & Brown, D. (2002). *Life Values Inventory* (Revised ed.). Williamsburg, VA: Applied Psychology Resources.

Crace, R.K., & Brown, D. (2002). *Understanding your values* (Revised ed.). Williamsburg, VA: Applied Psychology Resources.

Crace, R.K. & Brown, D. (2006). Life Values Inventory. In N.J. Salkind (Ed.), *Encyclopedia of measurement and statistics* (Vol. 2). Thousand Oaks, CA: Sage.

Crace, R.K., & Hanrahan, L. (1993). Eating disorders. *Sport Psychology Training Bulletin*, 4(4), 1–8.

Crace, R.K. & Hardy, C.J. (1989). Dealing with precompetitive anxiety. *Sport Psychology Training Bulletin*, 1(1), 1–7.

Crace, R.K., & Hardy, C.J. (1989). Developing your mental pacemaker. *Sport Psychology Training Bulletin*, 1(2), 1–6.

Crace, R.K., & Hardy, C.J. (1990). Relaxation training. *Sport Psychology Training Bulletin*, 2(1), 1–7.

Crace, R.K., & Hardy, C.J. (1996). Sport psychology and the injured athlete. In E.J. Shahady (Ed.), *Primary care sports medicine* (pp. 669–680). Cambridge, MA: Blackwell Scientific.

Crace, R.K., & Hardy, C.J. (1997). Individual values and the team building process. *Journal of Applied Sport Psychology*, 9, 41–60.

Crawford, R. (2008). *The use of environmentally responsible design in the strategic visioning of new product development* (Doctoral dissertation). Retrieved from ProQuest Dissertations and Theses.

Davidson, P. (1993). *The relationship of lifestyle orientation and family environment to mental health: An exploratory study* (Doctoral dissertation). Retrieved from ProQuest Dissertations and Theses.

Doehring, C. (2013). New directions for clergy experiencing stress: Connecting spirit and body. Pastoral Psychology, 62(5), 623–638.

Dominiak, M.C. (2006). *Utilizing branding theory to explore the relationship between personal values and perceptions of nursing as a career* (Doctoral dissertation). Retrieved from Loyola University Chicago (Accession No. 109847193).

Dorval, C. (1999). *Relational values in women's career role* (Doctoral dissertation). Retrieved from ProQuest Dissertations and Theses.

Dunning, D. (2010). *Contextual influences on career values* (Doctoral dissertation). Retrieved from ProQuest Dissertations and Theses.

Ercegovac, I.R., & Koludrovic, M. (2012). life values and divorce: Intergeneration and family perspective. *Sociology and Space*, 50(2), 257–273.

Frank, L. (1995). *Psychological and legal considerations in the assessment of decision-making capacity of older adults* (Doctoral dissertation). Retrieved from ProQuest Dissertations and Theses.

Fritz, M. (2015). *Knowing their values: A phenomenological study examining undergraduate leadership students' values clarification* (Doctoral dissertation). Retrieved from ProQuest Dissertations and Theses.

Galassi, J.P., Crace, R.K., Martin, G.A., James, R., & Wallace, L. (1992). Client preferences and anticipations in career counseling: A preliminary investigation. *Journal of Counseling Psychology*, 39, 46–55.

Galassi, J.P., Martin, G.A., Crace, R.K., & James, R. (1992). Guiding assumptions, data, and minor pestilence. *Journal of Counseling Psychology*, 39, 66–70.

Grunnet, U. (2013). *Women's voluntary midlife career transition* (Doctoral dissertation). Retrieved from ProQuest Dissertations and Theses.

Hamilton, S.B. (1989). Relationships between the life values of U.S. college students and their cognitive/affective responses to the threat of nuclear war. Journal of Adolescence, 12(1), 55–68.

Hardy, C.J., & Crace, R.K. (1989). Effective goal setting. *Sport Psychology Training Bulletin*, 1(3), 1–7.

Hardy, C.J., & Crace, R.K. (1990). Dealing with injury. *Sport Psychology Training Bulletin*, 1(6), 1–8.

Hardy, C.J., & Crace, R.K. (1990). Improving individual effort in team sports. *Sport Psychology Training Bulletin*, 1(4), 1–6.

Hardy, C.J., & Crace, R.K. (1991). Social support within sport. *Sport Psychology Training Bulletin*, 3(1), 1–8.

Hardy, C.J., & Crace, R.K. (1991). The effects of task structure and teammate competence on social loafing. *Journal of Sport and Exercise Psychology*, 13, 372–381.

Hardy, C.J., & Crace, R.K. (1993). The dimensions of social support when dealing with sport injuries. In D. Pargman (Ed.), *Psychological bases of sport injuries* (pp. 121–144). Morgantown, WV: Fitness Information Technology.

Hardy, C.J., & Crace, R.K. (1997). Foundations of team building: Introduction to the team building primer. *Journal of Applied Sport Psychology*, 9, 1–10.

Hardy, C.J., & Crace, R.K. (Eds.). (1997). Team building [Special issue]. *Journal of Applied Sport Psychology*, 9(1).

Hardy, C.J., Burke, K.L., & Crace, R.K. (2005). Coaching: An effective communication system. In S. Murphy (Ed.), *The sport psych handbook: A complete guide to today's best mental training techniques* (pp. 191–212). Champaign, IL: Human Kinetics.

Hardy, C.J., Crace, R.K., & Burke, K.L. (1999). Social support and injury: A framework for social support-based interventions with injured athletes. In

D. Pargman (Ed.), *Psychological bases of sport injuries* (2nd ed., pp. 175–198). Morgantown, WV: Fitness Information Technology.

Hebb, L. (2005). *Value similarity and satisfaction in interpersonal relationships* (Doctoral dissertation). Retrieved from ProQuest Dissertations and Theses.

Hogan, L. (2015). *The role of values in psychotherapy process and outcome* (Doctoral dissertation). Retrieved from ProQuest Dissertations and Theses.

Horley, J., Carroll, B., & Little, B. (1988). A typology of lifestyles. *Social Indicators Research, 20*(4), 383–398.

Hsieh, C.-L. (2006). *A study of the relationship between work values and career choice among hospitality management students in Taiwan* (Doctoral dissertation). Retrieved from ProQuest Dissertations and Theses.

Jordan, A. (2013). *A cluster-analytic approach to understanding the life values of North Carolina public alternative school teachers* (Doctoral dissertation). Retrieved from ProQuest Dissertations and Theses (Accession No. ED564740).

Kachgal, M. (2004). *A qualitative exploration of the career stories of novice women faculty in counseling* (Doctoral dissertation). Retrieved from ProQuest Dissertations and Theses.

Lautigar, D. (2002). *An exploration of career and lifestyle behaviors within the context of college student development for undergraduate female family and consumer sciences students* (Doctoral dissertation). Retrieved from ProQuest Dissertations and Theses.

Lerner, M., & Lyvers, M. (2006). Values and beliefs of psychedelic drug users: A cross-cultural study. *Journal of Psychoactive Drugs, 38*(2), 143–147.

Ligon, J. (1985). *Personality, subject area, time in service, and instructional methods: A test of Holland's theory* (Doctoral dissertation). Retrieved from ProQuest Dissertations and Theses.

Lips-Wiersma, M. (1999). *The influence of 'spiritual meaning- making' on career choice, transition and experience* (Doctoral dissertation). Retrieved from ProQuest Dissertations and Theses.

Lyvers, M., & Meester, M. (2012). Illicit use of LSD or psilocybin, but not MDMA or nonpsychedelic drugs, is associated with mystical experiences in a dose-dependent manner. *Journal of Psychoactive Drugs, 44*(5), 410–417.

Madsen, T. (2014). *Evaluation of a leadership program's impact on participants and civic engagement* (Doctoral dissertation). Retrieved from ProQuest Dissertations and Theses.

Meilman, P.W., Crace, R.K., Presley, C.A., & Lyerla, R. (1995). Beyond performance enhancement: Polypharmacy among collegiate users of steroids. *Journal of American College Health, 44*, 98–104.

Melin, L. (2015). *Being and becoming: An exploration of student spirituality in the second year of college* (Doctoral dissertation). Retrieved from ProQuest Dissertations and Theses.

Mitchell, J.V. (1986). Relationships between attitudes toward higher education and life values. *Assessment and Evaluation in Higher Education*, 11(2), 93–104.

Moorman, S. (2009). *Facing end-of-life together: Marital relationship quality and end-of-life health care preferences* (Doctoral dissertation). Retrieved from ProQuest Dissertations and Theses.

Oh, H. (2016). *A calling-focused career development program for college students based on Lasallian Spirituality* (Doctoral dissertation). Retrieved from ProQuest Dissertations and Theses.

Pisark, C.T, Rowell, P.C., & Currie, L.K. (2013). Work-related daydreams. *Journal of Career Development*, 40(2), 87–106.

Prince, J.P, Chartrand, J.M., & Silver, D.G. (2000). Constructing a quality career assessment site. Journal of Career Assessment, 8(1), 55–67.

Ringler, I. (2008). *Values satisfaction and participation in a community leadership program: A case study* (Doctoral dissertation). Retrieved from ProQuest Dissertations and Theses.

Rosenfeld, L., Wilder, L., Crace, R.K., & Hardy, C.J. (1990). Communication fundamentals: Active listening. *Sport Psychology Training Bulletin*, 1(5), 1–8.

Salkind, N.J. (2007). Quality of well-being scale. *Encyclopedia of Measurement and Statistics* (pp. 532–533). Thousand Oaks, CA: Sage.

Sandhu, G. (2014). *The influence of family and cultural values on the career development of Asian Americans* (Doctoral dissertation). Retrieved from ProQuest Dissertations and Theses.

Scammahorn, R. (2014). *Assessment of secondary agricultural educators' attrition risk in the southern region of the National Association of Agricultural Educators* (Doctoral dissertation). Retrieved from ProQuest Dissertations and Theses.

Schapiro, M. (1991). *Women preparing to reenter the workforce* (Doctoral dissertation). Retrieved from ProQuest Dissertations and Theses.

Shean, G.D, & Shei, T. (1995). The values of student environmentalists. *The Journal of Psychology*, 129(5), 559–564.

Silva, J.M., & Crace, R.K. (1987). *Psychological assessment of the United States men's national Team Handball team.* Technical report made to The United States Team Handball Federation (400 pp.), Colorado Springs, CO.

Silva, J.M., & Crace, R.K. (1988). *Interactive sports simulation system with physiological sensing and psychological conditioning* (U.S. Patent #4,751,642). Washington, DC: U.S. Patent Office.

Silva, J.M., Hardy, C.J., & Crace, R.K. (1988). Analysis of psychological momentum in intercollegiate tennis. *Journal of Sport and Exercise Psychology*, 10, 346–354.

Skopin, J. (1996). *The relationship between preservice teacher personality characteristics and the decision to teach at the elementary or secondary level* (Doctoral dissertation). Retrieved from ProQuest Dissertations and Theses.

Song, L., Li, X., & Li R.-C. (2009). An empirical research of life values of the Chinese post-80's youngsters. *Qingdao Daxue Shifanxueyuan Xuebao (Journal of Teachers College Qingdao University)*, 26(2), 21–27.

Steinmetz, M. (2017). *Examining the relationship between problem solving style and conventional, social, and enterprising career types* (Doctoral dissertation). Retrieved from ProQuest Dissertations and Theses.

Subramanian, S. (2001). Life values and perceived occupational stress among cosmopolitan (scientific) and local (administrative) – oriented scientists in R & D organization. Asia Pacific Business Review, 6(4), 74–81.

Subramanian, S., & Kruthika, J. (2012). Psychological factors determining high intentions to join defence services among adolescents. Journal of Organisation and Human Behaviour, 1(2), 39–45.

Taylor, J. (2014). *Environmental literacy development: A comparison between online and traditional campus courses* (Doctoral dissertation). Retrieved from ProQuest Dissertations and Theses.

Thul-Sigler, A. (2016). *the effects of career interventions on the career uncertainty of adults* (Doctoral dissertation). Retrieved from ProQuest Dissertations and Theses.

Unite, J. (2014). *A theoretical and practical application of the protean career: Do career skills and values training improve career decision-making self-efficacy* (Doctoral dissertation). Retrieved from ProQuest Dissertations and Theses.

Wanish, J. (2000). *An investigation of student development, life values, athletic identity, and the use of the center for enhanced performance among selected cadets at West Point* (Doctoral dissertation). Retrieved from ProQuest Dissertations and Theses.

Wekselberg, W. (1990). *Personality cognitive structures of work* (Doctoral dissertation). Retrieved from ProQuest Dissertations and Theses.

Wroblewski, S. (1992). Commentary on the utilization of the durable power of attorney for health care among hospitalized elderly patients. *ONS Nursing Scan in Oncology*, 1(1), 13–14.

Yavornitzky, P. (1997). *The effects of personality factors on value change in an inpatient psychiatric setting* (Doctoral dissertation). Retrieved from ProQuest Dissertations and Theses.

Zogmaister, C., Arcuri, L., Castelli, L., & Smith, E.R. (2008). The impact of loyalty and equality on implicit ingroup favoritism. *Group Processes & Intergroup Relations*, 11(4), 493–512.